THE NOwimpy PARENTING HANDBOOK

AN EASY GUIDE FOR RECLAIMING YOUR PARENTING POWER

KRISTEN C. WYNNS, Ph.D.

Layout and cover design by Kevin Wynns

ISBN: 1975848845
ISBN-13: 9781975848842

Library of Congress Control Number: 2017915574
CreateSpace Independent Publishing Platform, North Charleston, SC

Published by CreateSpace Independent Publishing Platform.

Printed in the United States of America.

At the time of this book's publication, all facts and figures cited are the most current available. All phone numbers, addresses, and website URLs are accurate and active. All publications, organizations, websites, and other resources exist as described in this book, and all have been verified. The author and publisher make no warranty or guarantee concerning the information and materials given out by organizations or content found at websites, and we are not responsible for any changes that occur after this book's publication. Content found in this book, NoWimpyParenting.com, WynnsFamilyPsychology.com, and other related resources is only meant to provide general information. It should not be used as formal psychological counsel.

To Kevin, my co-warrior in this No Wimpy Parenting battle

(and the love of my life), and Zoe and Logan, my girls,

who are good sports (most days) about being

the kids of the No Wimpy Parenting founder.

I love you guys!

Contents

Acknowledgments

It is hard to believe it's been six years since I was inspired to create the No Wimpy Parenting movement. Since then, I have presented dozens of No Wimpy Parenting workshops and coached many parents at my private practice in North Carolina. Of course, as with any monumental revolution, success does not rest on one pair of shoulders. I have been blessed with an amazing support network, without whom this book never would have come to fruition.

First, I have to thank my husband, who happens to be a top-notch graphic designer, logo creator, and website guru. He not only designed the eye-catching No Wimpy Parenting logo but also helped design our website, book, and related promotional materials. Never did I realize almost nineteen years ago when we married how complementary our careers would be. (He also designed my practice website and marketing materials, about which I get constant compliments and rave reviews.) Kevin, thank you for often delaying your own career dreams to ensure I could make mine come true. I love you!

I want to give another shout-out here to my girls, Zoe and Logan. Zoe is an author herself, having self-published three books by the time she was fourteen years old. Her hard work and dedication to churning out her books were quite inspirational to me, and our shared love of writing is so exciting to me. She gave helpful edits to this book that even the professional editor missed! Logan is our artistic one, but she was sweetly encouraging of my need to hole up in a room to finish this book. I love you, ZoLo! Thanks also to my parents and sisters, who have been supportive of my career dreams and writing this book.

To the first readers of my draft, who responded to my desperate request to "please read this ASAP and give me feedback" with enthusiasm: Dr. Korrel Kanoy; Dr. Sara Salter; my twin, Leigh; my mom, Kat; my kid, Zoe; my friend and parent of three, Theresa Ballinger; and a new author friend, Marilyn Lipman Shannon.

I am very appreciative of my amazing team at Wynns Family Psychology. Without my clinicians and admin team doing what they do so well, I wouldn't have the freedom to step away from some of my clinical work to write this book. I give a special thank-you to my clinical director, Dr. Sara Salter, who not only has taken a huge amount of stress and work from my plate but as a bonus, has become one of my closest friends.

This book is the result of some of the stories and successes I have experienced with my clients at Wynns Family Psychology. It takes guts to admit you are not a perfect parent and even more courage to drag yourself to a professional and ask for help. I happen to think my team at Wynns Family Psychology and I have the best clients in the world, and witnessing such positive responses from my clients helped propel this book forward.

Finally, I have to thank God for blessing me with so much! As a believer, I give God all the glory for any gifts or successes I have. God is at the center of my family, my marriage, my career, and my life.

Introduction: Starting a Revolution, One Parent at a Time

What is No Wimpy Parenting anyway?

About six years ago, I was sitting outside my daughter's gymnastic class with all the other moms, half reading a magazine, half people watching. I observed a harried mother trying to wrestle her child into the proper tights and leotard. As the child whined and fussed and pulled the "wet noodle" routine, the mother started warning, "Madison, you better straighten up, or we'll have to leave." Then a minute later, she said, "Madison, stop that, or we will leave." And then, "Madison, I'm telling you, we're going to leave if you don't behave." Fast-forward: Did they leave? Nope. Mom eventually dressed the child herself and promised her ice cream afterward if she'd go on into class. As I watched from behind my magazine, I was struck with how familiar that routine was. As a child psychologist, I had a parade of parents coming in for consultations to help with oppositional children, defiant children, disrespectful children, kids who just won't listen, kids who only do what they want to do, and teens who have no regard for rules. These parents were good people who really were trying. But they had no tools or strategies to keep (or gain) power in their own homes. In a broader sense, there seemed to be an epidemic of children and teens running the show as parents appeared to be helpless on the sidelines. As a mom of two, I could fully empathize with the struggle to consistently and effectively parent their kids the way they wanted. Even with my fancy degree and years of training, I was aware of how difficult it was to maintain control and authority in a home with children, who are naturally wired to want it their own way. As I watched the exhausted mother in the gymnastics class settle into her chair with a beleaguered sigh, I thought to myself, "There has got to be a better way. I should start a revolution to help parents get their power back. I want to light a fire in parents' hearts and minds to parent in a confident and successful manner. I want to end wimpy and ineffective parenting for good." In that moment, the No Wimpy Parenting philosophy was born. While No Wimpy Parenting started as a philosophy, it eventually transformed into tools and strategies I shared in parent workshops and with my parent-coaching clients. Finally, I became inspired and passionate about spreading the word (literally) to a wider audience, so all parents could transform their homes. Thus, I began working on this No Wimpy Parenting handbook.

"Why is this book so small and red?" you ask. "It doesn't look like the other parenting books around it at the bookstore or library." Glad you asked! Although I am a major bookworm and lifelong learner and could have stayed in school forever, I realize I have a certain love-hate relationship with self-help and parenting books. I have bought dozens of them through the years to address concerns I had as a mom or to inform my work as a child psychologist. I have a lovely stack of these books on my bedside table and on my bookshelves at home and at the office. How many of those books have I read cover to cover? Drum roll...zero! I have found most parenting books have way too many words and not enough user-friendly tips and are simply too clunky to stuff in a purse and read on the fly. Thus, I created a book that I would actually read! Cool, eh? My hope is that you, too, simply want a handbook that can be easily thrown into your purse or briefcase and read cover to cover in a couple of days or a week. I hope you have pages turned down that you want to reference again and again. I want this to be a parenting book that is read over and over and used as a resource, not just as a cool oversize coaster on your bedside table. Oh, and red is the color of No Wimpy Parenting because it's strong, powerful, and vibrant, just like you will be when I get done with you!

My mission is to recruit one parent at a time for the No Wimpy Parent revolution. Before you put this book under the pile of self-help books on your bedside table because you don't like where it's going, hang with me for just a few more minutes. No one wants to admit to being a wimpy parent. And for most of us, if we really acknowledge and confront this issue head on, we feel a jambalaya of feelings such as guilt, disappointment, frustration, anger, sadness...oooh, yuck! Put the lid back on! We'd rather just pour a bunch of rice on top to cover up those unpleasant feelings. But guess what happens if you don't nip these problems in the bud now? My experience is that these problems only get worse when your kids are older, taller, stronger, and hairier. Trust me. We are all in this together. I'm not a perfect parent by any means. As you journey through this book, you will read some stories from the trenches of the Wynns family that will show you that even a child psychologist's home is not immune to these issues. While I'm marching out in front pointing out important battle sites, yelling out commands, and singing a cool rhyming song we can march to in unison, I want you to know that when we cross the finish line of No Wimpy Parenting, we will all finish together as a proud pack of parents! So recruits...ready to join?

(Imagine a catchy military marching song as you flip to Chapter 1: "I don't know, but I've been told [I don't know, but I've been told], Wimpy Parenting is getting old [Wimpy Parenting is getting old], Hup, two, three, four. Hup, two, three, four!")

Note: If clients are referenced, all confidential and identifying details have been removed. Any other examples of children are made up (unless I claim them as mine).

1

Five Steps to Taking Back Your Power

Before we jump into the five steps, let me address a few possible elephants in the room. You may be asking yourself, "Is this No Wimpy Parenting (NWP) approach right for me?" Maybe you're a single parent or a divorced parent, and you're wondering if you can benefit from these tools. The answer is absolutely yes. In fact, as a single or divorced parent, you likely have additional stressors on you and challenges in parenting. Being armed with a simple and powerful bag of parenting tools will allow you provide a stable and predictable home for your children. Any tip or strategy you read about in this book can be used by parents in a two-parent home, a blended home, or a single-parent home.

Perhaps you are worried that because your child has special needs, or a childhood disorder, that these strategies won't work for you. While you may need additional professional help if your child has significant behavioral, social, or emotional issues, NWP is absolutely still an effective parenting approach.

You might even feel like it's too late and your family is in such distress, there is no hope for turning things around. Although there are no 100 percent guarantees, I can assure you if tackle this book with the intent to better understand your kids and adopt more effective strategies for parenting, things will get better. (Oops, did I just give a guarantee after all?) In all seriousness, parenting is very hard work, and it's exhausting. I have had many parents in my office fighting back tears (or letting them roll down their cheeks) despairing and feeling like they are the only ones having such a difficult time with their children. They feel all alone and guilty that they often don't even like their own kid anymore. I can tell you with confidence: You. Are. Not. Alone! This book is for you, and you can get out of the dark and hopeless place and move to parenting with confidence, happiness, and peace.

You may also be thinking, "Isn't this just authoritarian parenting with a focus on 'my way or the highway'?" Rest assured, although the NWP approach is certainly meant to

remind parents that the natural state within a home should
be parents maintaining authority and power and children
respecting that hierarchy, the NWP philosophy is not about
parents winning and kids losing. In fact, ~~if~~ **when** you make it to
the end of this book, you will have absorbed tips about instilling
a perfect balance of authority/power with love and connection
in your family.

A final disclaimer/tease: Once you begin to grasp the nature of
power in the home, you will be amazed at how you see dozens,
maybe hundreds, of examples of constant powergrabs by your
children and teens on a daily basis. In fact, you may be tempted
to start a punch card, like your favorite coffee shop has, and
make a notch every time you note another one. Clients and
workshop participants tell me with astonishment that they had
no idea how many instances occur every day, until they learned
about NWP.

To focus on the tenets of No Wimpy Parenting, let's begin with
an overview of the five steps to taking back your power.

FIVE STEPS TO TAKING BACK YOUR POWER

Step 1: Take the quiz: "Have I given away my power?"

Otherwise known as "Am I actually (gasp) a wimpy parent?" Check the boxes that apply.

☐ When you ask your kids to do something, do they frequently say, "No, because..." or "First I'm going to..." or "I can't because..."? In other words, do they typically not comply right away?

☐ Do your kids throw tantrums or get furious if you won't take them where they want to go, buy them what they want, or help them with something? Hint: Even teens throw tantrums; the tantrums just look a little different. If your teen fumes and fusses if you have restrictions on phone use, give a curfew, or tell him he can't go out tonight, that's a check for this question.

☐ Do you often find yourself threatening and warning repeatedly until you're so frustrated you lose your temper or give up on your original request?

☐ Do your kids make decisions about what they will and won't attend, when they'll go to bed, or when they'll turn off the TV or computer at night?

☐ Do your kids or teens ignore or laugh at your rules? (Even if you say there's a curfew or a bedtime, it's not really enforced, and the kids know it.)

☐ Do you often feel frustrated at the lack of respect you get from your kids? Do you feel like, "My kids do what they want to do and don't ever listen to me?"

☐ Do you dread going out in public because you're worried your child won't follow your rules or have a meltdown?

☐ Do you feel like you need to buy your child a treat every time you venture out on a grocery run for fear he or she will throw a temper tantrum in the checkout line?

☐ Have you ever felt so discouraged and upset over your children's behavior that you just wanted to give up?

If you answered yes to most of these questions, keep reading! This book is for you. If you happened to respond no to these questions, congratulations! You are already a card-carrying member of the No Wimpy Parenting movement. Order one of our No Wimpy Parenting bumper stickers to mount on your car, and then give this book to a friend or family member who needs some help.

Step 2: Reflect on "How did this happen?"

Good news: it's not all our fault. The cultural trends of modern parenting are much to blame. Some of the current popular philosophies of raising and educating children are disastrous for our families. Many of us were told "Give your children freedom" and "Let your children make decisions; it's good for their self-esteem." As a result, we have allowed the child too much freedom and put the child in control. In the era when every child gets a trophy, we have conveyed the wrong message to children about the ways of the world and what real life is like. Yes, we are encouraging our children to be free, assertive, and empowered. But this child-centric focus is not always helping kids build character or develop healthy resilience. Our current culture can overemphasize the idea that kids are at the center of the universe. Just look at the shirts kids wear these days that say, "There is no awesome without me" or "I am my favorite princess." Yes, these shirts can be harmless, but many parents are not teaching children enough about limits and discipline, hard work and perseverance, or empathy and respect. Experts over the last several years have advised parents, "It's good to give your child lots of choices," but we've taken that mentality to an extreme. In this era of helicopter parents, many have been encouraged and perhaps pressured by the modern culture to be overly helpful in preparing the path for the child rather than preparing the child for the path. As a generation, many parents have gone out of their way to give children most, if not all, of what they want to ensure no child is disappointed or, heaven forbid, has to endure chores, rules, or limits he or she doesn't like. It doesn't help that many parents carry guilt for having to work outside the home, and guilt can sometimes spawn a desire to overindulge the child or spare him or her from any negative emotion.

I often use the dirty diaper metaphor with my parent-coaching clients to explain this phenomenon. Remember when (for some of us, it was a looong time ago; for others, it may have been this morning) you would lay your baby down to change a dirty diaper? If your kid was like mine, she would often cry or wriggle as she was laid on her back and you went to town wiping that dirty heinie and putting on the clean diaper. Even if your baby cried, you would never have dreamed of stopping the diaper change. You would tell yourself, "Well, she has to have a clean diaper. I am being a good parent by giving this child a dry diaper and cleaning her plump little bottom." So you tolerated her tears, knowing that the bigger picture was of you doing the right thing as her parent. Fast-forward a bit to that same adorable tyke as a six-year-old. When that child is crying because she really wants the candy in the checkout line or because she desperately wants ten more minutes on the PlayStation, why do the rules change? Why do we think, "Oh no, she's crying and upset; that means I'm doing something wrong as a parent? Must. Make. Tears. Stop." No! Same rules apply. Sometimes when you are a being a good parent, your child will cry (or yell or fuss or whine or beg). No Wimpy Parenting strategies are going to remind you why this is OK and even good.

Step 3: Fill up your water gun (i.e., redistribute the power) "How is parenting like a water gun fight?" you ask. Imagine that when your beloved bundle of joy is first born, you are each issued a water gun. Each water gun is full of water, ready

for battle. Water = power. As you face your first parenting showdowns with your little one (usually when the child is about two), you start to develop some dribbles and leaks in your water gun in the following hypothetical scenarios:

1) Your toddler whines and cries for a lollipop in the checkout line at the grocery store. You hand it to him because people are staring and murmuring, "A little sugar never hurt anyone," and your dumpling is starting to cry louder. Water leaks out.

2) Your angelic princess refuses to put on her shoes for preschool, even though you've told her three times. You sigh and say, "Come on, let's go," and put on her shoes for her, then herd her out the door. Water dribbles.

3) Your first grader refuses to eat the vegetables on his plate. After you beg and plead and threaten, you agree he can have a cup of apple juice instead. Drip drop.

4) Your ten-year-old is happily playing video games. You remind her that electronics time is up for the day, and it's time for chores. She squeals, "But I need five minutes to get to the save point!" and continues to play. You sigh and say, "You and your video games! We're just gonna get rid of them some day!" as you walk out of the room, giving her additional time. Water leak.

If this happens enough, you will eventually have an empty water gun. Then guess what happens when you come face to face with your teen in the living room with your water guns raised when the stakes are really high (e.g., you need your teen to arrive home by curfew, abstain from underage drinking, or tell you the truth about where he or she is going)? Your teen will look at your empty water gun and laugh, thinking, "What are you going to do?" You both know you don't have any ammo left. Your water tank is drained, and on an emotional level, that's often how you feel, too.

(Note: This metaphor is not to imply violence or gun fights are a desired component of parenting. It is not about winning and losing. However, this visual is meant to illustrate how seeds are planted when children are young. If you want your teen to respect you and have a healthy fear of your authority, they have to know from many experiences you are locked and loaded, and that your parenting arsenal is fully functional.)

What are the common pitfalls that trip up parents every day, allowing their children and teens to have power and draining your water guns?

• **Many parents argue too much.** They go on explaining the same thing dozens of times because the kids continue to verbally poke, prod, and debate. Kids and teens are amazingly adept at sucking you into a verbal sparring match. Before you realize it, you have spent five minutes explaining why she has to shower every day, and she has delayed showering, which was her goal. It's wonderful for our children to learn verbal debate skills and to express their opinions, and the discipline literature does suggest children do better if they understand why they are being asked to do something. However, there is a time and a place for that type of discussion (e.g., if you are discussing the election, if you are planning a family vacation, or if you are deciding where to go for dinner), as opposed to a one-time command with a brief explanation (e.g., "We have an early morning, so please go ahead and pack your lunch tonight"). Arguing with your child when you have a clear idea of what he or she is supposed to do is a form of wimpy parenting. A helpful rule of thumb is "first time, every time." That means it is the family's expectation that when a parent asks the child or teen to do something, the child obeys immediately and doesn't engage you in a long argument. Hint: you will learn more about this with CWC (command, warning, consequence) in Chapter 3.

- **Lack of follow-through.** If you say, "If I find your shoes in the living room again, I'm going to donate them to Goodwill," donate them to Goodwill if you find them again. Once your children know that you will do as you say, then you won't have to do it as much. They will respect your word.

I had a parent-coaching client who eventually became a poster parent for NWP. Her eleven-year-old son, Chip, who saw me for therapy to help with ADHD and behavior problems, had a sense of entitlement, often slacking off on his daily responsibilities. His mother threatened that if he didn't properly do his chores that week, they were going to give away

his brand new, super-trendy basketball shoes. When Chip continued the bad habits that week, she drove him to one of the Goodwill donation boxes in a parking lot. Chip had to get out of the car and make the long walk to drop his beloved shoes in the giveaway box. Although the mom (and I, actually) felt a pang over this, what an impact this made on Chip. He knew his mom meant what she said, and he couldn't hope she was bluffing. Note: The discipline literature would suggest it's best to try the mildest action that will work and then go stronger if needed. With this example, it may have been enough to remove the shoes for a week before donating them.

• **Too many choices!** Yes, it's good to give kids choices. However, in the present day, it seems parents often give the illusion of a choice when deep down they mean something is mandatory. They ask the teen if she wants to go to her therapy session this week or if he wants to stay after school for cross-country practice. Parents shouldn't be asking kids, "Do you want to go to bed now?" or "Do you want to go to church today?" If it's something you want your kids to do, make it a statement: "Time for bed." "We leave for church in ten minutes; be ready." In addition to phrasing commands as commands and not questions, it's important to have a clear sense of what activities or items you are fine with your child choosing. I advise parent-coaching couples to discuss together what activities are mandatory in the home and which they will allow the child or teen to choose. For example, parents may agree that church, therapy, music practice, school, and family birthday parties are mandatory activities. They may also insist that kids eat some fruits and veggies every day, drink milk, and have a set bedtime. However, they may decide that their children can choose which sport to play each season, what clubs they join at school, when to wake up on weekends, and what to pack in their lunches every day.

Shortly after I created No Wimpy Parenting, we had our pastor and his wife over for dinner. As we ate, I excitedly told them about the NWP movement and philosophy. After dinner, as we relaxed in the living room, I realized time had gotten away from us, and it was close to our girls' bedtime. I turned to my girls and said, "Do you guys want to get ready for bed now?"

Both girls shook their heads and said, "Nope."

I had to laugh, as did our guests, as we realized the irony of the request. I looked knowingly at our guests and said, "Let me try that again. Girls, it's time for bed. Please go brush your teeth and put on PJ's." Thankfully, both girls immediately hopped up and marched into the bathroom.

Step 4: Maintain the new power structure

We will unpack these ~~weapons~~, um, tools, in more detail in chapter 3. But the following simple yet highly powerful tips are going to serve as the foundation of your new No Wimpy Parenting plan:

- **Follow through with consequences.** If you ground your child from his phone for a week, don't let him have it back in two days because he's harassing you for it. If you put your child in time-out for four minutes and she giggles and runs away in two minutes, bring her back again. See punishments through. I often joke with parents that children are natural gamblers. They will roll the dice every time to see if they can get a winning combination to hit the jackpot. (Forgive me if I am blurring casino and lottery terms. I have only spent about thirty minutes in Vegas up to this point.) It's also important not to threaten a consequence that you know will end up ruining your day or weekend or that you will regret, unless you are confident you can remain firm.

When our oldest, Zoe, was about nine years old, she struggled with some disrespect and sassing issues. We had been trying to rein in this misbehavior, and when the problem continued to escalate, I warned Zoe that she would lose "sweets" the next day if she had another incident of mouthing off. She continued to have that "tween 'tude" so she got grounded from sweets. Well wouldn't you know, the next day was our North Carolina State Fair. (Side note: I have a sweet tooth and love seeing my children experience wonderful, tasty treats.) The next day, it was torture for Zoe (and us, to a lesser degree) to see her little sister and parents gobbling up caramel apples, cotton candy, and deep-fried Oreos. Although we felt tempted to throw in the towel and say, "OK, that's enough. Go ahead and have a bite," we held firm. Our willingness to see this consequence through had a positive impact on our daughter in the long run (and her little sister, who had a front-row seat to the aftermath). She realized we meant business.

- **Keep it simple.** Don't try to focus on too many behaviors and issues because it will overwhelm you, and you won't end up following through on anything. Choose the top three to five behaviors you struggle with, and try your best to correct and discipline those behaviors every single time. If you give negative remarks and reprimands for everything, your discipline will lose power.

  For example, let's say you have a high-energy child who loves to run through the house while chasing the animals and whooping a war cry. This child also sasses you, refuses to stay in bed at night, and breaks his sister's toys. To prioritize, you can let go of his yelling and running (for now) and focus on him speaking respectfully, staying in bed, and treating property with respect. If children are constantly corrected and reprimanded, your discipline will become diluted and less effective as your child simply learns to tune you out. It's also important to phrase behavioral goals in the positive rather than the negative. For example, if you have an aggressive child and you ask him to stop hitting his sister, he has to first visualize hitting and then mentally cross that out. Phrasing it this way actually forces the child to focus (for a second or two, but it does make a difference) on the undesired behavior. However, if you ask him to use his words and keep his hands to himself, he visualizes the positive behavior you desire of him.

- **Beware the dreaded "power suckers"!** (More on this in the next chapter.)

- Pushing your buttons. Most parents have no idea how powerful it is for the child or teen when the parents lose their temper or yell and scream. When kids can push your buttons and get you to erupt, these explosions give kids a massive surge of power!
- Negotiations (e.g., "Well, I'll eat the carrots if I can get ice cream later") or asking questions (e.g., "Why do I have to brush my teeth?"). Before you know it, your child has launched into a ten-minute dissertation about why she has to brush her teeth even though kids in Africa don't have toothbrushes, and brushing teeth wears off enamel, and so on.
- Partial compliance. Kids may try to cut corners instead of giving 100%. It's important not to accept this as close enough; insist on full compliance.
- Questioning and decision-making. Kids telling you what they are and aren't willing to do...small things eventually add up to filling up their water guns and depleting yours.
- Ignoring you or refusing to cooperate when you make small requests.

Step 5: Avoid regression to the old ways

Many parents enthusiastically embrace new parenting strategies and do a great job for a couple of days, maybe a few weeks. Then reality hits...long days at work, tired parents, and smart kids. Parents lose their resolve and get sucked into the bad habits again. How do parents avoid the vicious cycle of on-again, off-again parenting plans? Even if you implement the following tactics for the first few weeks, these ideas will help you know you are not alone and remind you to track your positive progress.

- Find an accountability partner—whether it's your spouse, a parent, or your best friend. You need someone who will ask you daily, "How are you doing with Billy? Are you still following through? Are you still being consistent? Are you correcting his behavior every time he misbehaves?" Share with this person as many specifics as you can. Explain your parenting goals and the strategies you are implementing, and ask for direct feedback and challenges. It's ideal if you can arrange to meet in person for a weekly lunch or coffee to discuss your successes, setbacks, and new resolutions for the following week.

- Another suggestion is to keep a parenting log and at the end of the day, take five minutes to write a summary of the day. Include detailed notes about triggers for behavioral incidents or problems with the kids, as well as successes. Ideally, you would share this log with your co-parent and continuously fine-tune what specific techniques and strategies work best for your family.

- Seek additional help from a professional. If you and/or your co-parent are very stressed and overwhelmed, you may benefit from having a psychologist or coach check in with you to encourage and advise you. As we discussed earlier, it's also important to enlist the help of professionals if you or your child(ren) have additional emotional, social, or behavioral concerns. You may also want to seek out a customized No Wimpy Parenting consultation with the founder herself, and there are opportunities for that as well.

Finally, remember these techniques aren't to give your ego a boost or to wear your kids down. Kids need and want boundaries and limits. Knowing where the line is and exactly what you expect makes kids feel safe, secure, and loved. Although they may never admit it, kids and teens feel much less anxiety and stress when they have a sense of clear expectations and know parents are in charge. So know that what you're doing isn't just going to make you feel good; it will ultimately make them feel happy, relaxed, and proud, too!

FIVE STEPS TO TAKING BACK YOUR POWER

2

How to Avoid Power Suckers

I had a parent-coaching client (a single dad) who had three girls, ages sixteen, twelve, and ten. He was the CEO of a large company and had a seven-figure salary. By the time he came in for his initial consult, he was raw with emotion and exhausted physically and mentally. He confessed, "I have this high-level job overseeing five hundred-plus employees. I am ex-military. I have top level clearance with the FBI. And I cannot say no to my girls." Thus began the journey of this powerful, strong man realizing his girls were holding the power in the home, and his commitment to reset that power structure in the family.

Let's unpack steps three and four of taking back your power a bit more. After you've familiarized yourself with the steps to taking your power back, it's time to get serious about zapping power suckers in your home. Power suckers are those pesky and often sneaky things kids do that deplete parents' power over time. What many parents don't realize is that for most families, it is not one big face-off with your child or teen that causes problems. For most of us, it is a series of small, insidious, persistent, chronic (am I painting the picture yet?) incidents that eat away at the bond between parent and child and eat away at the soul (I mean stamina) of the parent. Power suckers are seemingly minor, alarmingly innocuous-looking behaviors of children that take away from your authority and respect as a parent bit by bit. These behaviors are the ones draining that water gun, a few drops at a time.

What are some of the common power suckers invading our homes?

Here are the top five power suckers:

1) Pushing parents' buttons (i.e., getting your goat)

I'm staring eyeball to eyeball with my twelve-year-old. A simple request to clean up the kitchen counters has resulted in rolling of eyes, whining, and begging to postpone. I give a warning: "If you don't clean this up now and stop talking, you're going to lose electronics for the rest of the day."

"Cool," she says, while slinking behind me to the other side of the kitchen.

How can one word set off so much emotion? My kid knew that if she said "Cool" in a flippant, disrespectful way when I was disciplining her, it infuriated me to no end. She had pushed my buttons and was now waiting for a (possible) explosion. From a scientific perspective, let's consider how emotions originate in the limbic (primitive) part of the brain but need to be transferred to the frontal lobe for calmer decision-making. When this doesn't happen, it's called hijacking in the emotional intelligence world, and we aren't thinking clearly anymore.

HOW TO AVOID POWER SUCKERS

Most children keep escalating their bad behaviors or ignoring you until you lose your cool (i.e., yell and scream), and allow your brain to get hijacked. I would say 99 percent of kids (made-up statistic based on clinical experience) learn over time exactly how to get a parent's goat. Some kids slam doors; some say, "Whatever"; and some can achieve the desired result with a rolling of the eyes and a sigh. My nephew says, "Yes'm" to get under his mother's skin. (It has the semblance of respect, but he tweaks it to make his point.) An NWP coaching mother described how her nine-year-old's bloodcurdling scream when she didn't get her way immediately set off a physical reaction in her own body. Her daughter knew her screaming would provoke Mom to scream and yell in response.

Here is a life-changing revelation for many parents: when you yell and scream at your child, you're giving away all your power. Think about how few things kids get to control in their young lives. They often have to go to school, brush their teeth, eat some veggies, do homework, and so on. But if they can say or do something and witness an immediate reaction on your part (turning several shades of a deep red, increasing the decibel level of your voice, having that wicked forehead vein bulge), wow, what a surge of power they feel. Kids get a sense of empowerment from pushing your buttons like that. When you lose your temper and allow them to see you lose control, it is ironically a very reinforcing sequence for your kids. And guess what? As with all reinforcing activities, kids then want to do it again and again and again.

2) Negotiations

Many parents have no idea how often they are sucked into negotiations with their child or teen. Really pay attention this week to how many times you make a request of your child, and he or she come back with a negotiation. For example:

Parent: *"Turn off your game, and wash your hands for dinner."*
Kid: *"First I have to get to the save point on this game, then I'll go."*

Parent: *"In ten minutes we're going to need to clean up and get ready."*
Kid: *"No, fifteen. I want to finish this show."*

Of course, as children turn into tweens and tweens into teens, the sophistication of the negotiations advance, too. Now getting your teen to accompany you to the grocery store becomes a five-minute discussion that ends in you promising a stop at Starbucks and purchasing her that new mascara she must have.

Negotiations may come across as innocent at first. You may even admire your child's intellectual prowess and think, "This kid will be a great attorney or mediator someday." To a certain degree, negotiating skills are a sign of verbal and cognitive smarts. However, if your kid's foundational belief is "Whatever my parents say can be modified if I simply ask in the right way or persist in alternatives," you've got a problem. In order to have a healthy balance of power, kids need to respect that what you say is the final answer, and there is no negotiating allowed. Negotiations can also be implied or subtle, but they are still a power-grabbing attempt. For example, one weekend morning when I was making waffles and mentioned to my daughter that I was going to add the dreaded chia and flax seeds, she said, "Oh, no way. Then I'm not eating them. I'll find something else" and went to the fridge. Now, I knew my homemade waffles were the superior choice, and instead of begging, "No, wait, I won't add them so you'll eat them," I cheerfully went about stirring my mix. Eoz (name changed to protect the innocent) went through motions of putting a frozen waffle in the toaster as I continued

my prep work. Seeing I was giving none of her antics any
attention, she asked, "Can I pick out the seeds?" I responded in
a very neutral, calm tone, "Nope, they're too small to pick out."
Eoz then removed the waffles from the toaster, put them back in
the freezer, and casually said, "Fine, I guess I'll have yours."

3) Partial compliance

This means your child does some of what you ask or starts to
comply but then doesn't fully obey. In other words, the child
settles for mediocrity or "good enough." For example, you ask
your child to feed the pets, and he goes to refill the cat's bowl,
neglecting to feed the dogs and fill the water bowls. Or you ask
the children to clean their rooms and discover the floor has been
picked up, but there are mysterious piles of junk in corners, on
dressers, and stuffed in the closet. "Well, at least they tried!" you
may be thinking. True. But remember, we are trying to shape
these creatures into functioning, competent members of society.
Do we want them to start their first job with the mentality of
"Let me give as little effort as possible and still appear as if I'm
trying my best"? Of course not! Partial compliance is dangerous
in that the child's response doesn't shoot your blood pressure
up right away as a "No! You can't make me!" response does.
Therefore, if you are off your game, these partial compliance
incidents may sneak by you unless you are on the lookout.

4) Questioning

Parents often spend a lot of time explaining to, rationalizing
for, and pleading with a child to make them understand why
they should do what the parents have asked. Although it's
certainly healthy for children to have a sense of curiosity and to
develop communication skills, when it comes to compliance and
obedience, the rule of thumb is "less talking and more action."
As a very wise man once sang, "A little less conversation, a little
more action, please. All this aggravation ain't satisfactioning me.

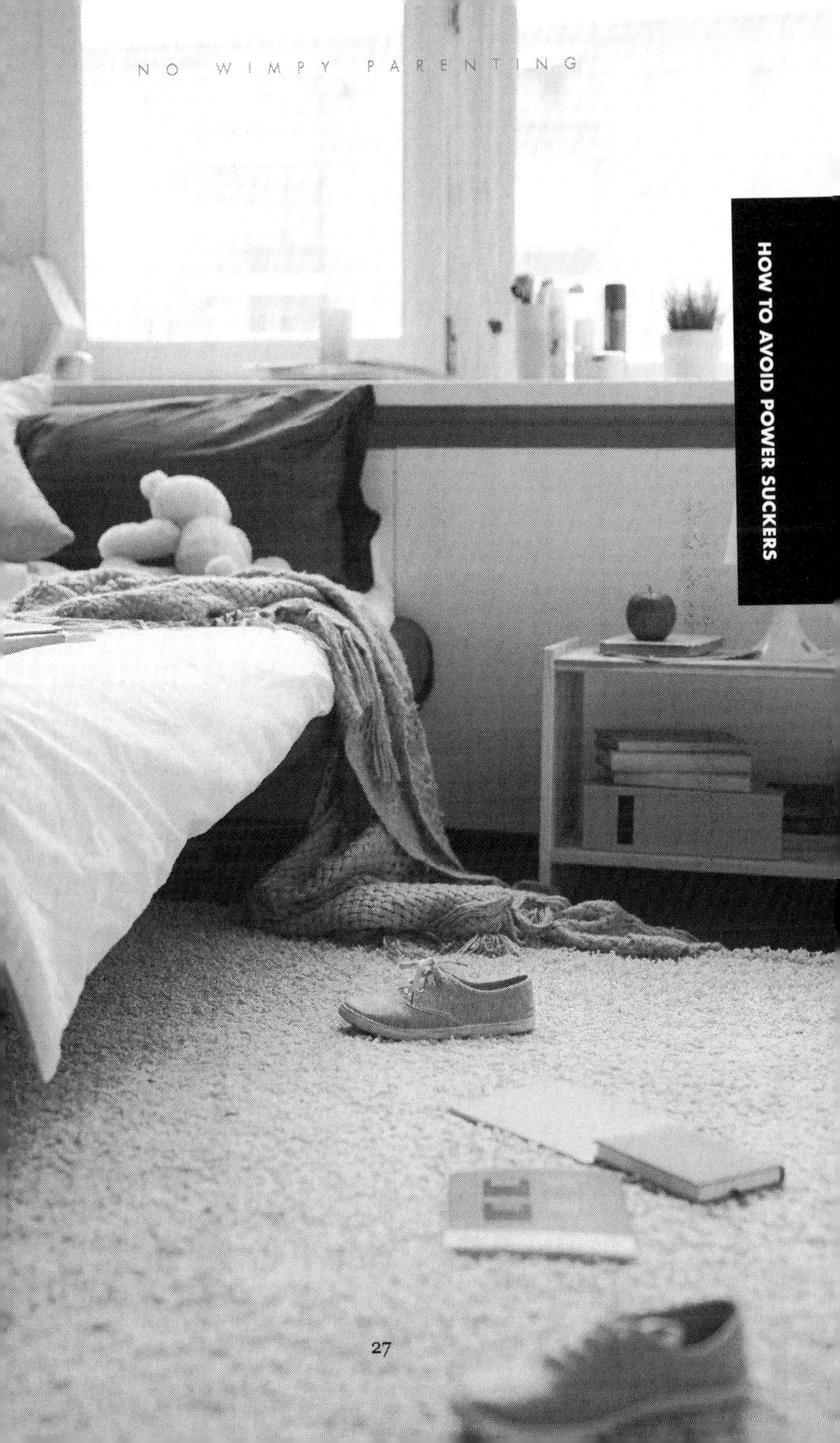

A little more bite and a little less bark." I know, I know, Elvis had something else in mind, but nevertheless, you should see the point.

Parents don't have to give a dissertation on why their child has to brush her teeth every night; it's enough to say, "It's healthy, and you have to do it." Questioning is similar to negotiation, but it feels like this:

Mom: "Hey, Danielle. Go ahead and unload the dishwasher before you go over to Madison's house."
Danielle: "But Mom, why do I have to unload it now? Why can't I unload it later? Actually, Jason hasn't done any of his chores this week, why can't he do it? And most of my friends have like, no chores at all. Why do you guys make us do chores every single day?"

Like negotiating, questioning is exhausting for parents if they don't shut it down in the early stages. I personally find I am weak and vulnerable a) in the morning before I have had my mandatory three cups of coffee and b) in the evening when I am watching the clock and counting down the minutes to children being in bed; looking forward to my laptop being closed for the night and snuggling on the sofa with my hubby, a cold beverage, and mindless reality TV.

5) Decision-making

Again, it's good for kids to make some decisions (e.g., cornflakes or oatmeal? Jeans or shorts?) But when a child expects to be able to make decisions about going to school, church, baseball practice, or any other commitment that the parents believe is important, that's unhealthy. I often hear kids say something like, "Well, I'm not going back!" (They may be talking about a social skills group, Boy Scouts, or piano lessons.) And the parents say, "OK, sweetie, if you don't want to go, we're not going to make you." Yes, it's OK to make your child go places. And yes, you can even carry your ten-year-old to the car if you have to. (Guarantee: it will only take one time carrying your child into an event to ensure he or she will comply and go from that point forevermore—in most cases, long before you walk in the door carrying him or her like a baby.) When children and teens believe they can decide if they will attend certain events or contribute to the house by doing chores, it sets an unhealthy precedent that is more dangerous as they get older. If they have learned they can decide for themselves, what happens when you tell them to be home at eleven o'clock and they decide they would rather stay out until midnight?

I had a parent coaching client who was genuinely on the edge of a nervous breakdown by the time she came in for services. Her seventeen-year-old was essentially holding the family hostage with his verbally abusive and manipulative behaviors. He refused to comply with any parental requests, and his parents and brother literally hid out on a different floor of the house most nights to avoid his wrath. When his mother and I decided psychological testing would be valuable to determine what was driving his difficulties, she knew he would refuse to participate because he was used to deciding what he would do and not do. While it took us three parent coaching sessions just to craft the plan to get him to the appointment, we had success! After Mom firmly connected his participation in the testing with his cell phone service and attendance at his beloved soccer games at high school (at which he was the team's star player) he showed up for testing. Being firm about this decision being in the parents' hands began to change the entire power flow in the home.

6) Bonus power sucker: ignoring

Ignoring parents is more common with younger children, but it is a very effective and destructive power sucker. To illustrate: one hot summer night, my family and I were at a party at a local neighborhood pool. An adorable little boy, about four years old and with a mischievous gleam in his eye, was frolicking in the shallow end. He caught my attention the first time because he was splashing my friend, who was in the water, with a naughty glint in his eyes. As the evening went on, I observed his father coming to the edge of the pool to speak to his son. The little boy would mightily splash his father, who was dressed in pants and a shirt. The father would glare at the son, yell something (I couldn't hear the exact words), and make a physical swipe to grab the boy. I witnessed this same scene at least five times! Each time, the father would ask the boy to stop or motion him to come out of the water. The boy would come just close enough to splash his father and then dive away, as his father reached out to grasp for him and pull him out. The father had no power, and the boy was clearly accustomed to ignoring his father's requests or commands. Even when the boy temporarily came out of the pool and stood next to his father, his father did not take advantage of this opportunity to lean down and speak to his son or have him sit out of the pool. He looked quite dejected and frustrated and simply watched as his son dashed off to jump back in again.

When children think it's a game when parents speak or make requests, it is a dangerous sign of problems to come. Children need to learn early on that each and every word that comes out of a parent's mouth is to be respected and responded to.

OK, so now that we have identified these pesky power suckers, how do we activate anti-sucking techniques? (I'm sure you won't find the phrase anti-sucking techniques in any other parenting

HOW TO AVOID POWER SUCKERS

book on the planet.)

1) Anti–button pushing

Keep your cool! No matter how good your child is at pushing your buttons, stay calm. If you have to remove yourself from the room to take a few deep breaths and give yourself a pep talk, do so. I encourage parents to imagine a shield of armor surrounding them. Everything the child says or does just pings off this shield, as you remain calm and cool underneath. It is a matter of you staying in control. Once you have taken a breath or stepped away for a minute, you return and firmly, but calmly, address the situation. Hint: in some cases, the way you remain in control is to let it go. Not reacting and ignoring can be very powerful (as with my waffle-making example). But never ignore egregious behavior such as cursing, saying mean things to you, or destroying property. If your children or teens learn that no matter what sassy or rude thing they say, you consistently react with a calm, cool, but firm response, the number of sassy comments will greatly decrease. You've taken the fun out of it for them. For really upsetting button pushing, you may need to remove yourself from the room or the house for a few minutes or more until you have gotten that heart rate back down, and you can talk without hissing or yelling. As a fringe benefit, children's behavior often improves when you remove the audience. Some kids and teens are wired for the power struggle and the adrenaline that comes from the fight. If you remove yourself as the audience, most kids feel pretty silly continuing a tantrum or meltdown.

There are tons of free relaxation resources online these days. Any exercises that emphasize deep breathing, guided imagery, progressive muscle relaxation, meditation, or mindfulness are great to keep at your fingertips. (On your cell or iPad is ideal, so you can step away, put in earbuds, and have relaxation going in less than sixty seconds.) Here are some of my favorite relaxation websites:

- **www.dartmouth.edu/~healthed/relax/downloads.html**
- **www.mcgill.ca/counselling/self-help/audio-video**
- **marc.ucla.edu/mindful-meditations**

There are even "quickie" relaxation strategies you can do with no technology or gadgets needed. One of my favorite easy techniques for both kids and adults is simply tracing up and down your fingers while inhaling and exhaling deeply.

Breathing Technique

TRACE ALL FIVE FINGERS

EXHALE

INHALE

START HERE

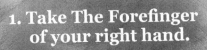

1. Take The Forefinger of your right hand.

2. Trace slowly around the edges of your left hand.

3. When your finger moves to the tip of the finger, breathe in.

4. When your finger moves towards the palm, breathe out.

2) Anti-negotiations

Aim for less talking and negotiating and more action. If a child is questioning you or arguing, give your final statement and remove yourself. Example: "I have told you that you can't go shopping today because your room is a mess and our schedule is too tight. This is the end of the discussion." If the child is being disrespectful and keeps pestering and harassing, give a warning. ("You can't talk to me that way. If you continue, you'll lose your electronic privileges today.") In general, try to consistently mean what you say, so your child learns that there is very little chance you will change your mind.

However, once you establish consistent beginner-level anti-negotiations, you can advance to level two and occasionally engage in negotiations. For example, if you ask your teen son to mow the lawn, and he asks, "Since it's so hot now, can I do my indoor chores and homework first and mow the grass after dinner?" you can see the logic and reasoning in his request. If you and he both know that what you say goes 99 percent of the time, it's fine to give him some wins, especially as he is becoming an independent human apart from you and moving toward adulthood. You can respond, "You know, Jack, that's a great idea. Why don't you finish up your room and bathroom? Then after dinner, you can scoot outside."

3) Anti–partial compliance

Don't accept less than the best! Don't accept a job that's half done just because you're exhausted and frustrated. If you set this precedent, your child will know he can give less than his best, and this trend may spill over into other areas of his life (e.g., school and work). If you see your daughter or son has only done some of what was asked, point out what is needed to finish the job and make sure it is done in a timely manner. You may consider tying in natural consequences to partial compliance. In other words, if your offspring conveniently forgot to put away the rest of the laundry, you can warn him that next time it isn't done completely the first time, he'll need to take over the folding of the clothes, too.

I have observed in my own family that partial compliance can quickly become a very bad habit. I noticed that most of the time, when I gave one of my girls a chore, it would not be completed. When I asked my daughter to clean the counters in the kitchen, I found a salt container, bowls, random key hider containers, and so on. When the little one was asked to sweep, I found telltale evidence of crumbs, fur balls, and plastic clothing tags in the corners of the rooms. Because this issue got so out of hand, I instilled a zero-tolerance policy around it. In other words, if they were busted with a "half-butt effort" (my daughter coined this phrase), they automatically earned twenty to thirty more minutes of chores.

4) Anti-questioning

Remind yourself that your child will often use questions and discussions to avoid doing what you've asked them to do (in other words, keep a bit of power for themselves). The longer they keep you talking, the longer they delay doing what you've asked. If you're like me, and you often have between twelve and fifteen competing thoughts at any moment, you may also end up very distracted and even forget your original request. So keep discussions around commands short and sweet. It's OK to say, "We'll discuss this later, but for now, go ahead and do what I've asked." If it's not a command but a decision your child is questioning, you can use a similar approach, saying, "Your dad and I have discussed this at length. We don't feel comfortable with you going to that camp this summer, and our decision is final."

5) Anti–decision-making

Specifically tell your child which things are up for discussion and which are nonnegotiable. Example: "Mom and Dad want you to go to church and Boy Scouts each week. We'll let you choose which sport you want to do in the spring." If your child tries to say what he or she will or won't do, remind the child which things are nonnegotiable. Consider the following: family birthday parties, religious activities, work-related events, Boy/Girl Scouts, music lessons, therapy/doctor's appointments, sports practices/games, and other extracurricular activities. If your child pushes back against the mandatory activities, just respond briefly with why the activity is mandatory. ("When you commit to a sport, your team is counting on you, and you need to see this season through.") You may also want to remind the child of the activities he or she does have freedom to choose. ("Remember, you can choose if you want to sign up for another year of art club at school.")

If you are in a two-parent home, I strongly advise that you and the other parent sit down and agree on the nonnegotiable activities. If you are divorced and attempting to co-parent cooperatively with your ex (good for you, by the way!), I advise you to have the same discussion via e-mail or in person if you are amicable. Explain to your ex that you would like to have consistent expectations for your children, and determine if you can come to a consensus on what is considered mandatory.

6. Bonus: Ignoring

How to handle ignoring? Easy! Don't ignore ignoring. 😃
If you ask your child to do something, and he or she doesn't respond, immediately repeat the request or statement again, remembering the three keys to effective communication with kids or teens:

1) Eye contact: Make sure you are face to face with your child, and neither of you has a device in front of your face.

2) Proximity: Ensure you are close to your child or teen. I am guilty of shouting a request upstairs or across the house and then being frustrated when my daughter doesn't respond or gets it wrong. I know it's a pain, but take the extra minute to go and get in front of your child.

3) Tone of voice: Make sure it is firm and loud but not yelling.

After checking off the three keys to effective communication, you are free to move on to CWC in the next chapter!

HOW TO AVOID POWER SUCKERS

3

Three Little Letters to Transform Your Parenting:
CWC (and Bonus ZTB)

Anyone who has worked with me for a while knows I love acronyms and metaphors. In fact, my twin and I both mightily defend our claim that we are the inventors of JIC (just in case), as in "Let's bring our umbrella JIC." (You are free to start using that; just please give the credit to Dr. Kristen Wynns.)

Are you ready for an acronym that can truly transform your home in a matter of days? CWC: command, warning, consequence. Remember that characteristic of wimpy parents who keep making a request and weakly giving a warning over and over and over? CWC is going to nip that in the bud. Here's how it works:

1) Give the command: "Zoe, please get your lunch packed for school, and then get your book bag ready to go."
   a. If Zoe marches off to pack her lunch and grabs her bag, all is well. Nothing else to do.
   b. If Zoe keeps checking messages on her iPad and grumbles she'll do it later, move to the next step.

2) Give a warning: "Zoe, I asked you to pack your lunch and get your book bag ready. If you don't do it now, you'll lose iPad time after school."
   a. If Zoe gets up to pack her lunch and grabs her bag, all is well. Nothing else to do.
   b. If Zoe whines, "I said I'd do it later, geez!" and walks into another room to finish her message, move to the final step.

3) Announce the consequence: "OK, Zoe, you chose to disobey when I asked you to pack your lunch and grab your bag. Now you have no iPad time after school today." (Remember, a key component of CWC is to follow through on the consequence, so you would need to set an alarm or write a sticky note reminding you she has no iPad after school.)

If this magic formula seems way too easy, it's because it is! Most parents cycle CWCWCW or CWWWWW endlessly. In other words, they avoid giving the consequence at all costs. Why? It's no fun to give consequences and punishments. As parents, we are hardwired to want happy children. Happy children = happy parents. However, at a certain point, parents must realize that a happy child at the expense of appropriate parenting and discipline leads to an unhappy family down the road. I often use this example to explain to parents why our goal should not always be to avoid an unhappy child or teen.

Remember the diaper-changing example? Recall that image of your baby screaming her little head off at times during diaper changes because she hated to be on her back. Your baby was clearly sad and mad and unhappy with your actions. But you kept changing her diaper because you told yourself, "This is the right thing to do. She has to have a clean and dry bottom, so I gotta persevere." When we fast-forward to big-kid, tween, or teen years and that same adorable child is now crying and mad, it doesn't necessarily mean you need to stop what you're doing. Your child may be upset because you are being a good parent, and that's OK! Tell yourself the same thing you did when she was crying as you brushed her tiny infant teeth: "This is the right thing to do. I am being a good parent. This is good for her."

Many of my parent-coaching families have told me CWC is one of the easiest yet most powerful tools they have encountered. Many came back after one or two weeks of consistently using CWC, exclaiming, "We can't believe how effective it is. Our kids are now obeying the first time we ask them to do something."

ZTB: Zero-tolerance behaviors

One couple client of mine had a feisty seven-year-old who was fond of cursing—not just the minor, kind-of-cute-because-he's-so-small cursing but the dropping-f-bombs-on-a-regular-basis kind of cursing. When this family implemented CWC plus the ROCKS system (you'll learn about this family more in later chapters), their son stopped cursing altogether within a few weeks. When this couple, who had great senses of humor, learned about certain behaviors having automatic consequences (zero-tolerance behaviors), they cleverly adopted ZTBs in their home. (With their permission, I have stolen this acronym to use with my No Wimpy Parenting folks.) ZTBs modify the CWC formula in that some behaviors are just so bad, so egregious, such no-no's that they require automatic punishments or consequences. Examples of ZTBs are hitting, biting, destroying property, cursing, or running away. It's important to explain to your children and communicate with your spouse or co-parent about the ZTBs for your family and to spell out what the consequences are. For instance, you might tell your tween any time he yells at you, he automatically loses his electronics for the next twenty-four hours. Or you might explain to your little one that any time he hits his sister, he has an automatic time-out. As we discussed earlier, it's critical to be choosy when identifying ZTBs, or the concept loses its potency. Decide which acts or behaviors are truly the worst of the worst, against your family's (or society's) values, or dangerous, and designate those as ZTBs. Ensure your kids are told in advance what behaviors are ZTBs, so they aren't caught off guard when you announce, "OK, you slammed your door. Hand over your car keys."

4

How ROCKS Can Revolutionize Your Reward System

Over the years, I've developed a behavior modification system for kids involving actual "rocks," so naturally I tried to create an easy-to-remember acronym...

R.O.C.K.S.—Reinforce Our Children–"Karrot" System...
(Well, I tried.)

How can a jar filled with decorative rocks (the ones you find with vases and jars at crafty stores) decrease negativity, improve listening, enhance cooperation, and drastically overhaul your children's motivation to behave? How can dangling a "karrot" motivate children and teens to transform their behavior? Answer: when those rocks become currency to "buy" everything your children hold dear and love in their world. Many parents

are giving away so many freebies to their kids on a regular
basis, when these freebies are actually privileges to be earned!
Examples of such privileges include the following:
- TV and video game time (screen time)
- having a cell phone
- having texting and social media on their phones
- social outings with friends
- dessert or treats
- new toys or games
- the newest Converses or name-brand jeans
- events like going to the movies, to a trampoline park, to an
  arcade, et cetera.

Many families provide these privileges simply because a child
is breathing and takes up space in the universe. I like to remind
parents that the only freebies kids are truly entitled to are
food, shelter, education, hugs and kisses, love, and clothes (not
name-brand, top-of-the-line clothes, but something to cover
your naked body with kind of clothes). Therefore, parents
need to reconfigure the structure in the home and recalibrate
expectations of the young folks by explaining, "Hey, guys. We
are going to be using a new system in our home in which you
have to earn your privileges from now on." List them, then
wait for a few minutes to allow for moaning, groaning, and
gnashing of teeth. Then explain the fun part: "I know, I know.
This is a little different. But guess what? You guys can help us
brainstorm the rewards you want to add to the system." Then
go on to list the privileges you've already thought of (dessert,
electronics, social outings, etc.). But then enlist your kids' help
in brainstorming customized extras for each child. For example,
your eight-year-old daughter may ask, "Well, how many rocks
would it take to buy a new American Girl doll?" Or your tween
son may ask, "How many rocks would I need to have a friend
go with me to the skateboard park?" As kids get creative and

dream big, they realize this new system may not be all that bad. I have truly been amazed at how quickly behavior improves in my home when we are consistently using the ROCKS system. (I will admit, we don't use it 365 days a year because as things stabilize and improve, we can often back off the system for a while, using a looser system of rewards and consequences.) Out of all the strategies or tools I have shared with my parenting clients through the years, ROCKS is without a doubt the strategy about which I have received the most overwhelmingly positive, family-transforming feedback. If we are in a lull, my own kids will even ask to start using the ROCKS system again because it makes earning things and saving money very matter of fact. For example, we translate one rock to ten cents in our house. So if my kids have a debt they are working off or if we are going on vacation and they want spending money, they are highly motivated to earn rocks. (They even ask for bonus opportunities to earn more...more on that later!)

When learning about the ROCKS system, many parents tell me, "I'm against rewarding kids for good behavior. Kids should do the right thing just because. I shouldn't have to reward every little thing." My response is typically twofold: First, I explain that for many kids, intrinsic motivation isn't consistently in place until much later in childhood and adolescence. While you hopefully see traces of intrinsic motivation for some behaviors (usually ones that are more meaningful to the child like sports, grades, or building the next world in Minecraft), it is unusual to observe children naturally motivated to behave all the time.

Secondly, as adults, most of us partake in a reward system called the paycheck. Even though I love my job and happily skip to work most days, I also expect and am motivated by the money I earn. Providing children a reward mirrors real life and is effective as a short-term strategy as you are training and shaping behavior. However, note the key phrase short term. The ROCKS system is meant to be a living, breathing system in the home that evolves constantly with your children. Once a reward has been paired with a behavior or chore for a while and you note consistent success, it's important to remove that reward and aim for a different, more challenging goal. For example, if your child was earning rocks for her morning routine but is now brushing her teeth, combing her hair, and getting dressed easily every day, you would eliminate rocks for that behavior, and move on to packing school lunch. If kids (or adults, for that matter) are rewarded for every behavior, the reward loses its power. Explain this concept to your children as you are moving the rewards to a new target behavior.

If you are ready to implement ROCKS in your home, here is your starter kit:

1. Have a meeting with your spouse and any other adults in charge at home. All parents and guardians need to agree to the same plan with the same consequences and rewards. It is extremely important to keep a behavior plan consistent across caregivers and settings.

2. List target behaviors you want to see more of. These start behaviors may include the following:
    - obeying the first time he's asked—first-time-every-time obedience
    - speaking to parents in a respectful tone
    - using words when angry (expressing feelings appropriately)
    - daily chores or hygiene tasks like brushing teeth
    - completing homework independently within a certain time limit, with a good attitude

Then list stop behaviors, ones you want to eliminate, including the following:
- no whining
- no hitting/punching/pushing (physical aggression)
- no yelling/screaming
- no destruction of property
- no forgetting homework or materials for school

For younger kids or when targeting chores, make a list of the child's daily activities, and be specific. This should include everything the child does in his or her daily routine—for example, waking up, brushing teeth, getting dressed, eating meals, playtime, naptime, and so on—all the way until bedtime. Choose a few gimmes for the start behaviors that will be easy and hopefully guaranteed ways of earning rocks each day.

3. Of all the behaviors you listed, pick the top five behaviors you want to see more of (one or two chores in here are fine) and the top five behaviors you want to see less of.

4. Allow your child to be a part of implementing the behavior plan. Let him or her pick out and decorate a rock jar or some other type of container with stickers, glitter, ribbon, and so on. Make sure you specifically outline what positive behaviors are and what negative behaviors are. Including your child in the planning and implementation of the plan will make him or her more likely to cooperate.

5. Get decorative rocks at Target, Walmart, or Michaels (any craft store will have them), the kind you put in vases with flowers. You can also use marbles, small tokens, or coins.

6. For each positive behavior, assign the number of rocks that can be earned. For each negative behavior, assign the

number of rocks that can be taken away. For more important
behaviors, assign more rocks (four or five), and for easy
chores, assign a smaller number (two or three).

7. Select six or more rewards or privileges that are desirable to
your child. List these rewards on a sheet that can be posted,
and assign each privilege a rock value, depending on how
special or desirable that reward is to your child. Rewards may
be getting a toy, going to see a movie, getting a treat, and so
on. When choosing rewards, make sure you include some that
can be achieved daily as well as some that make take a week
or more to complete.

- Examples of daily small incentives: X amount of TV or
  video game time, X amount of phone or computer time,
  dessert, staying up fifteen extra minutes, et cetera.
- Examples of medium incentives: trampoline or bouncy
  house venue, renting a movie, picking the restaurant,
  getting ice cream, a "date" with Mom or Dad, a trip to
  the dollar store, a medium-priced toy, a sleepover, etc.
- Examples of big incentives: expensive toy or clothes,
  expensive outing like an arcade or adventure park,
  buying a new video game, getting a new pet.

8. For each positive behavior, allow your child to place the
appropriate number of rocks into the rock jar. For the first
two or three weeks, only focus on positive behaviors; do not
take rocks away yet. (Parents are always eager to get to taking
away, but the idea of only earning rocks the first few weeks is
to have the child buy into the system and get excited about it.
After a couple of weeks, begin to take rocks away for negative
behaviors. By this point, your children or teens should be very
motivated to earn rocks, as they have seen the perks of this
system. When they realize they can lose rocks, they should be
appropriately horrified, while at the same time motivated to

continue good behavior.

9. Your child can cash in rocks at any point to receive a reward. It is important for your child to have frequent feedback, so make sure he or she can easily receive a reward within the first week or so of implementing the behavior plan.

10. You are encouraged to award bonus rocks if you feel your child has displayed a good behavior that is not on the list of positive behaviors. For example, if your child offers to help you unload groceries from the car, watches a younger sibling for you, or helps you in the garden, you may want to compliment the positive behavior and offer up extra rocks.

11. Remember to stay consistent and hold your child accountable for every positive and negative behavior. Don't save up for the end of the day, reviewing and giving or taking away rocks then. It should happen as immediately as possible.

12. Wait for the spike. With almost any new parenting strategy, you can expect to see children's behavior tank and become even worse. You might think, "This is crazy. They're worse than they ever were when we didn't do any of this." Please, hold on. Don't give up, as this is to be expected. When kids or teens sniff out a change like this, consciously or not, they are going to behave worse in an attempt to make you give up on this new parenting plan, which seems scary to them because they might not be in control anymore. So stay the course, ride out the spike, and wait for the reduction in the poor behavior that is guaranteed to come!

13. It's ideal to share your ROCKS plan with grandparents, babysitters, and even teachers (at least goals that relate

HOW ROCKS CAN REVOLUTIONIZE YOUR REWARD SYSTEM

to school). The more caregivers and involved adults
understand and reinforce this system, the better!

FAQs/Troubleshooting

1) So, the first few weeks, we just let them get away with bad
behavior?

No. It is important to still correct negative behaviors in your
normal way while you are reinforcing the positive ones.
Removal of privileges and time-outs are the most appropriate
and effective means of disciplining for negative behaviors
such as hitting, disrespectful language, or noncompliance.
Physical means of punishment such as spanking are
ineffective for long-term changes in behavior and only result
in short-term compliance out of fear. Physical punishments
also often exacerbate a child's aggressiveness or anger
problems. See chapter 5 for more creative discipline methods.

2) What if we are out at the grocery store or at church? How do
we do ROCKS if we are on vacation?

The beauty of ROCKS is that it is easy to transport and easy
to implement wherever you are. For younger children, you
can transport a plastic baggy of rocks in your purse. For
older tweens and teens, you can simply have a notebook with
notch marks for tracking positive and negative behaviors and
transactions for rewards.

3) I know my twelve-year-old. She will think rocks in a jar are
stupid and babyish. How do I get her on board?

You can customize the system to match your child's age and
preferences. Your tween or teen may want to track behaviors
on a dry erase board or in a spreadsheet on the computer. As

HOW ROCKS CAN REVOLUTIONIZE YOUR REWARD SYSTEM

long as the basic tenets of the system are followed, you can tweak it to fit the needs of your family.

4) My kids are going to freak when we tell them they now have to earn video games, YouTube time, and outings with friends. They may revolt!

Yes, it's true. When parents first introduce this new system, the first reaction from children may be lukewarm at best and outright hostile at worst. However, once kids and teens realize a few key factors, they tend to come around. Specifically, when kids realize they can get creative and add other events, toys, or games they want to the rewards menu, they get excited about ROCKS. When they understand they control the system and, as long as they are behaving and doing what they need to do, they can keep getting more and more rocks, they feel empowered. Finally, as a bonus, this system takes away some of the emotion and taking it personally of parenting. Instead of a child or teen blaming a parent for a punishment, the parent defers to the ROCKS system. It's the agreed-upon system, and it becomes more matter of fact than when parents are handing out rewards and punishments randomly. This is a big advantage for parents who have less relationship damage using this type of system than they do using willy-nilly parenting.

5) Should I include grades in ROCKS?

There is a decent amount of research suggesting that incentivizing grades does more harm than good. I typically advise parents to reward behaviors related to good grades such as turning in homework on time, dedicating a set amount of time to studying, keeping desks and book bags organized, and doing homework independently rather than rewarding the actual grades.

Sample ROCKS Behavior Plan

Child's Name: _____ Start Date: _____

Positive/Start Behaviors* ☺

Behavior	Value	Sun.	Mon.	Tues.	Wed.	Thur.	Fri.	Sat.
1.								
2.								
3.								
4.								
5.								
Total Points								

Negative/Stop Behaviors ☹

Behavior	Value	Sun.	Mon.	Tues.	Wed.	Thur.	Fri.	Sat.
1.								
2.								
3.								
4.								
5.								
Total Points								

Rewards and Privileges	Value	Sun.	Mon.	Tues.	Wed.	Thur.	Fri.	Sat.
1.								
2.								
3.								
4.								
5.								
Total Points Spent								
Total Points Remaining								

What might this plan look like in an imaginary family with an inattentive ten-year-old boy named Adam, who has an aggressive streak?

Sample ROCKS Behavior Plan

Child's Name: **Adam**   Start Date: **10/14**

Positive/Start Behaviors* 😊

Behavior	Value	Sun.	Mon.	Tues.	Wed.	Thur.	Fri.	Sat.
1. Pack book bag and lunch	3		3	3		3		
2. Use words when upset	5	5					5	
3. First-time obedience	5		5	5		5		5
4. AM routine independently	3	3	3	3	3	3	3	3
5. Turn in homework	5		5	5	5	5		
Total Points		8	16	16	8	16	8	8

*Keep in mind, on a typical chart, he might get rewarded for some of these behaviors multiple times per day.

Negative/Stop Behaviors 😦

Behavior	Value	Sun.	Mon.	Tues.	Wed.	Thur.	Fri.	Sat.
1. Hitting	-10				-10			
2. Name calling	-5			-5				
3.								
4.								
5.								
Total Points				-5	-10			

Rewards and Privileges**	Value	Sun.	Mon.	Tues.	Wed.	Thur.	Fri.	Sat.
1. 30 minutes video games	20	-20					-20	
2. Candy	5			-5	-5		-5	
3. Stay up late 20 minutes	10						-10	
4. New video game	150							
5. Outing to skateboard park	250							
Total Points Spent		20		5	5		35	
Total Points Remaining								

**Adam "bought" rewards using banked rocks from prior weeks.

5

Time-Out
(Dusted Off and Polished)
& Other Creative Consequences

If I had a dollar (or a rock) every time someone said "Time-outs don't work for us," I would already be on my private island in the Caribbean by now. The fact is, many parents are not properly implementing time-outs. There are a few essential ingredients to a flawless time-out:

1) Explain the time-out process in advance. When your child is calm and you have time, sit down and talk about what to expect if he or she has to go to time-out. Explain how he or she will be warned, the expectation of how many minutes, and the necessity of sitting in the time-out spot the entire time without talking. Finally, make sure your child knows that when the time is up, you will come and discuss the incident and have him or her apologize.

2) Don't forget the warning. In most circumstances (with the exception of a ZTB), you need to specify what undesirable behavior is occurring and warn the child that if it continues, time-out will occur.

3) Yes, it's true. The right amount of time is one minute per year of life. Although some treatments like PCIT recommend specific lengths of time, most child-development specialists encourage one minute per year of the child's age. Therefore, if your child is four, time-out should last four minutes. (When my oldest was thirteen, she laughed when I threatened a thirteen-minute time-out, and yes, you would typically find other means of punishment beyond age ten.)

4) Choose the right place. Time-out needs to occur in a quiet and boring but open place, preferably with no distractions. Good examples are a chair in a corner of the room, a special mat, a stool, or a bottom step. The point is you should be able to keep an eye on your child, without having to physically keep him or her in the chair. That leads me to...

5) Do it the right way. Time-out does not mean you are holding your child in your lap or restraining the child in the chair. Although there are some circumstances in which you may need to more actively hold your child in place, your child should remain seated on his or her own.

6) Safety first. If you need to use a room for time-out, ensure there is nothing dangerous in the room your child can get into. You should also never use a closet for time-out or turn off the lights. You don't want to scare your child you want to remove him from the fun and give him a chance to reflect on his behavior.

7) If your child gets out of the chair or placement, the time starts over. You should have an egg timer, stop watch, or sand timer visible to your child. There are even digital sand timers and timing devices on apps and online, such as http://www. online-stopwatch.com/eggtimer-countdown/full-screen/.

8) If your child talks to you, yells, screams, or gets out of the chair, you start the time over. You do not engage with your child in any way other than to calmly say, "We have to start the time over."

9) Once the time is up, get eye level with your child and ask, "Why were you in time-out?" Once she gives a reasonable, age-appropriate explanation, ask her to apologize. Once she apologizes, give her a hug and move on with your day. If the child refuses to apologize or speaks in a rude way, provide another warning about the need to apologize or speak respectfully, or the child will need to spend additional time in time-out. Finally, it's helpful to have the child correct the misbehavior if possible. For example, if she threw a toy in anger, have her replace it on the toy shelf.

To address what-if scenarios, let's look at one disastrous and one ideal time-out.

Scenario 1

Little three-year-old Mason has been irritable all morning. After being told to stop throwing toys near his sister, he continues to throw toys. His harried mother shouts, "That's it; time-out for you." She puts him on a nearby sofa and continues to play with his sister.

Mason screams, "That's not fair!" and slides off the sofa and runs toward the kitchen.

His mother chases him, and once she catches him, she gently tosses him back on the sofa and says, "I told you, it's time-out!" When he begins to cry, his mother says, "Crying isn't going to change anything. You never listen to me, and you're gonna hurt your sister someday." Mason, now very upset, hops from the sofa again, running toward the back door. As he is trying to escape outside, his mom swats his behind, screaming, "You do not go outside!" Mason cries harder now and collapses in a child-puddle on the floor. Mom scoops him up, hugs him, and says, "You better be a good boy the rest of the day, you hear?" Mason runs off to play, while an agitated Mom rejoins little sister on the floor to play.

What went wrong? Oh, where to start. A few of the noteworthy mistakes:
- There was no warning.
- There was no timer or telling the child the amount of time he had to sit.
- The mother engaged in conversation, yelling, and physical punishments in the middle of the time-out, instead of calmly walking Mason back and restarting the clock.
- The mother sent mixed messages by grabbing the child and hugging him, then sending him off to play after he had just been reprimanded. Mom also forgot about, or gave up on, any attempt at a time-out.

Scenario 2

Let's peek at another family with Dad, Mom, six-year-old Chloe, and four-year-old Charlie. The Adams family is enjoying a wonderful dinner of fried chicken, corn on the cob, and green beans. Chloe is getting wild and silly at the table, using her corn cob as a weapon to wave in Charlie's face. Dad verbally corrects Chloe, saying, "Chloe, table manners, please." Chloe continues to joust with the corn cob, so Dad says in a firm voice, "Chloe, if

TIME-OUT (DUSTED OFF & POLISHED) & OTHER CREATIVE CONSEQUENCES

you don't stop playing with your corn, you will go to time-out." Chloe sheepishly lowers the corn cob but then uses it to smack a funky beat on her plate. Dad states, "OK, Chloe, you were warned about the corn. Now you will go to time-out." He pulls Chloe's chair out for her and gestures to the time-out chair in the living room, saying "Six minutes." He follows her, setting a timer app on his cell phone, and places the phone on the coffee table within eyeshot of Chloe.

As he heads back to the table, Chloe giggles and sprints back toward the kitchen. Her father goes after her, saying, "Chloe, time-out starts over because you left the chair. Come back and sit down."

Chloe whines, saying, "I'm just playing. You're mean!"

Dad ignores this, gently prodding her back to her chair and resetting the clock. He joins the rest of the family at dinner, while keeping an eye on Chloe. When the timer goes off, Dad leaves the table, squats in front of Chloe, and asks, "Why were you in time-out, Chloe?"

Chloe responds, "Because I was playing with the corn on the cob and you said not to."

Dad prompts her: "What do you need to say?"

"I'm sorry," says Chloe, reaching up to her dad for a hug.

Her father hugs her back, and states, "OK, come back and finish your dinner, so we can all have ice cream."

Hey, nice job, Adams family! What all did Dad do right?

- He gave a very specific warning about an inappropriate behavior.
- He followed through with sending the child to time-out immediately after the infraction.
- He set the timer for the appropriate amount of time, keeping it within sight of the child.
- He reset the timer when Chloe escaped time-out.
- He did not respond in any way when Chloe got upset and started talking to him.
- After the time was up, Dad had Chloe say why she went to time-out and apologize.
- After a hug, life resumed, and he did not hold a grudge or continue lecturing her about the offense.

Chores

Hands down, chores are my favorite consequence/punishment. Why? Chores are a win-win. Your child or teen has to do

TIME-OUT (DUSTED OFF & POLISHED) & OTHER CREATIVE CONSEQUENCES

something unpleasant and not fun, while you get something crossed off your personal to-do list. Chores are especially effective with older elementary kids and teens. Sometimes parents send children to their rooms as a consequence, but we all know that lying on your bed and chilling isn't that bad a deal. In fact, I would love to be sent to my room to rest for 42 minutes. (One minute per year, remember?) However, if a child or teen uses those same ten to thirty minutes actively doing a chore, the impact is much greater.

How does this work? Like a time-out, you give a warning for the inappropriate behavior: "Josh, the way you are speaking to me is completely disrespectful and offensive. If it continues, you are going to go outside and pull weeds for twenty minutes." If Josh continues to mouth off, say, "OK, Josh, you were warned. I am setting the oven timer for twenty minutes. Take this trash bag, and go pull weeds. I'll come notify you when time is up, so you can throw away the bag after I inspect it and clean up." When Josh is finished with the chores and standing before you, sweaty and dirty, ask, "OK, Josh, why did you have to pull weeds?"

Josh begrudgingly says, "Because I was rude to you. I'm sorry."

You give him a fist bump (because, well, he's sweaty and dirty) and send him on his way.

What are some chores to give children and teens?
- Washing and drying dishes
- Loading and unloading the dishwasher
- Folding clothes or matching socks
- Sweeping or mopping
- Bathroom duty
- Pulling weeds
- Watering plants, the lawn, or the garden

- Special projects like organizing the Tupperware cabinets or pantry, cleaning out the fridge, washing the car, cleaning the garage, or painting your toenails. (All right, I threw that one in there to make sure you were paying attention.)

As a bonus, you can use chores to punish and alleviate sibling issues. We found when our girls were fighting with each other and we gave joint chores such as folding laundry together or organizing the cabinets, they would weirdly unite against us. By the end of the chores, they'd be laughing and bonding as they worked and had forgotten why they were mad at each other.

You may be wondering, well, shouldn't kids and teens have chores anyway? Yes, absolutely! Most child psychologists, including myself, believe chores are an important part of developing responsibility and instilling a work ethic in children. I recommend that most families have a few daily and weekly age-appropriate chores for each child. Our children are currently fourteen and eleven. Each girl has the following daily chores:

- Cleaning bedroom and bathroom (picking up, making sure sinks aren't nasty with toothpaste, hanging up towels, etc.)
- Cleaning out cars (dragging in all their stuff from school or camp)
- Watering or feeding the cats
- Cleaning out and preparing book bags for the next day (school year) or camp bags (summer)

Each girl has two weekly chores that need to be done by 8:00 p.m. on Sunday:
- Unloading dishwasher
- Watering all plants inside and out
- Sweeping first floor
- Folding laundry for fifteen minutes (usually socks,

TIME-OUT (DUSTED OFF & POLISHED) & OTHER CREATIVE CONSEQUENCES

underwear, and towels)

What about allowance? Interestingly, although the topic of allowance seems to universally come up in most homes at some point, there is very little research on the pros/cons or best plans. Parents seem to fall into three camps:

- Allowance is "free." The child or teen gets X amount of weekly spending money just because, and there may or may not be additional expectations regarding spending, saving, or donating to charity.
- Chores earn allowance. Each child or teen has daily or weekly chores that must be completed each week to earn his or her allowance. A concern with this plan is a child may decide he or she would rather not do the chores and doesn't care about the money. If parents consistently encounter this type of issue, they may consider making some chores mandatory and adding a bonus system, so additional chores earn an allowance.
- No allowance. Some parents believe each member of the family is expected to contribute to the home by doing chores and embrace a communal-sharing philosophy. These parents typically provide for the child's or teen's needs by covering costs of outings, birthday gifts for friends, and the occasional toy or game a child might be coveting.

Through the years, we have experimented with the latter two philosophies. In our home, the chores = allowance seems most effective, but our children understand when the house is very messy, when we are hosting a party, or after vacation, we request additional help around the house just because, and they are expected to cheerfully pitch in. We also built in a second layer of defense by having daily chores as one of the checklist items in the electronics gauntlet. (You'll read about that in chapter 8.) Therefore, our kids are more motivated to complete daily chores so that they can earn electronics time.

Removal of privileges/grounding

Once your child ages out of time-out, it is typically good timing to introduce grounding/removal of privileges. Although having a positive behavior system such as ROCKS goes a long way, it's typically necessary to have a punishment plan in your home as well. For certain offenses, parents will find removing privilege of cellphone or videogames (or electronics altogether), taking away sweets, or grounding from social time with friends is a nice second line of defense to back up your reward system. As we discussed in earlier chapters, remember to make the consequence doable and reasonable. If you ground your teen from his phone for the rest of the year, chances are low that you will see this consequence through. Quite frankly, it is also hard to remember punishments if you make them last too long, as you have about 203 other things racing through your mind. Make the removal of privilege specific, with a set length of time, and make a note on your calendar or memo on your phone to remember the details. For example, if you tell your teenage daughter she loses her car privileges through the weekend and can get it back for school Monday morning, then mark your Google calendar with a "Laney no car" reminder every day of her punishment.

TIME-OUT (DUSTED OFF & POLISHED) & OTHER CREATIVE CONSEQUENCES

6

Go Team:
Presenting a United Front
with Your Spouse/Partner/Co-Parent

One of the primary sources of conflict for couples (after sex and money) is parenting disagreements. Frequently, parents become more polarized in parenting styles, discipline techniques, and expectations for children's behavior over time. The parent who is slightly more permissive becomes much laxer in the face of a parent who initially was slightly stricter but not extremely rigid. Couples feel they are constantly compensating for the other parent's weakness, and this lack of unity leads to a great divide between the parents.

On a day-to-day basis, many couples are constantly undermining the power and authority of the other parent. They may do it in subtle ways (e.g., "Did Daddy really say no TV for the rest of the night?") or overt ways (e.g., "Mommy is wrong. She shouldn't have let you stay up late like this. This isn't good. Go to bed!"). Parents may have frequent arguments about parenting and feel like they are individual parents rather than co-parents. This division leads to the couple feeling a lack of intimacy and being constantly irritated and stressed. Over time, spouses may even experience a lessening or loss of trust. When I work with parents in coaching sessions or in couple's counseling, I often hear similar complaints:

"He is the softy parent."

"She gives the over-the-top punishments but then forgets about them."

"I have to be the bad guy, and he gets to do all the fun stuff."

GO TEAM: PRESENTING A UNIFIED FRONT

Even in our home, we see how easily our children figure out the dynamics between us and which of us is softer on which topics. For example, our daughters know I am more relaxed and soft when it comes to clothing, boys (argh!), social media, the Internet, and girl milestones like shaving legs. The girls know that my husband is easier when it comes to bedtimes, screen time, video games, and junk food.

Many couples try to get on the same page by giving in to make their spouse happy. For example, a wife might say, "Fine, I'll be better about disciplining them. But you've got to stop screaming at them so much!" This type of pseudocompromise might work in the very short term. But without a more fundamental shift in individuals' perspectives about co-parenting and the need to present a united front, couples quickly drift back to bad habits. They may argue, criticize the other parent, try to get the child(ren) on their side, and sabotage the other parent's efforts to be a good parent. Parents may also ignore differences in parenting style in order to avoid a fight. However, this buried tension tends to erupt at some point. It is better to address this problem head-on.

What is the solution to this problem?

Consistency, consistency, consistency!
There are three types of consistency that help bridge the gap:

1) Consistency of rules

Explain your rules carefully and clearly to your children. Make sure they understand. Then explain the consequences for breaking each rule. Most importantly, enforce the rules and consequences consistently. Yes, that means each time!

2) Consistency between parents

Present a united front to your children. Co-parents need to communicate with each other about rules and consequences for the children. Children always look for a chink in their parents' armor, so make sure you agree on the rules. Children learn how to play one parent against the other, so parents should confer and agree on rules, requests, and discipline before sharing their decisions with the children.

3) Consistent routines

Many family events require routines: bedtime, chores, meals, bath time, and school mornings. Children love routines and predictable events although they might never admit it. When routines are consistent, children respond better. When there are no set routines and schedules, kids can sometimes feel anxious and out of sorts, even if they can't articulate why. Routines take the guesswork out of parenting.

If you don't already have a semblance of a routine, take ten minutes to map out a typical weekday and weekend schedule. If parents disagree about the schedule itself, find the middle ground. For example, what if one parent always sends the kids to bed at ten o'clock, while the other parent aims for an eight-thirty bedtime? Parents may decide to agree to a routine bedtime of eight thirty on school nights and ten o'clock on weekends; then they no longer have to feel divided on the issue. Or these parents may settle on nine-fifteen as a happy medium. Of course, as kids turn into tweens who turn into teens, routines may be relaxed.

Other tips to overcome the divide
- You and your spouse or partner need to be explicit with each other about what your rules and expectations are for the children. As mentioned earlier, don't try to conquer the world; just focus on the top five to seven behaviors, rules, or values you care about the most. It's helpful to write family rules down and post them on the refrigerator or on a family dry-erase board, review them, and be sure they are workable.

- In areas in which you differ, find a compromise you

both can live with and stick by it. If you truly can't find a compromise, it's best to defer to a professional with expertise in that area. For example, if you disagree about whether your children should consume artificial sweeteners, let your pediatrician break the tie, or see what American Academy of Pediatrics says on the subject. (Note: This is an actual debate in our home, and wouldn't you know the American Academy of Pediatrics (AAP) website says, "Due to limited studies in children, the American Academy of Pediatrics...has no official recommendations regarding the use of noncaloric sweeteners"? Well, that's not all that helpful, is it?)

Fortunately, if you and your spouse disagree about how old the children must be before they stay home alone, you can get a slightly more definitive opinion from AAP here: **www.healthychildren.org/English/safety-prevention/at-home/Pages/Is-Your-Child-Ready-To-Stay-Home-Alone.aspx**. (Short answer: experts agree on age eleven or twelve before a child can stay home alone.)

- You and your spouse need to commit yourselves to communicating about every significant issue in your family life. Ideally at least once a day, the two of you need to check in with each other and discuss what happened that day that was important. At the same time, talk about long-term issues that may be confronting the family. Even if you grab five or ten minutes on the back deck debriefing the day's events and trouble spots (e.g., John's excessive Xbox use, Jill's messy room), you will stay connected and on the same page about issues affecting your family. Longer-term issues would be discussing when to get your tween or teen's first phone, when to discuss sex with your

GO TEAM: PRESENTING A UNIFIED FRONT

kids, or handling an upcoming change in schools.

- You and your spouse need to resolve your own ambivalence on important family matters and agree on a position on these issues. For example, if one spouse is undecided about spanking, there may be conflict when the other one spanks. Research it, read up on it, seek the help of a professional, and then make a clear decision on the issue.

- Find ways to cooperate, not compete, with each other. That doesn't mean you have to agree on everything, but it does mean that you are committed to working together toward a more harmonious relationship and family life, and you are not going to let differences undermine your common goals. Each of you needs to demonstrate some flexibility.

- Like any good wrestlers, use the tag-team system. If your partner is engaged in an angry debate with your teen son and you can see he is about to lose it, use a prearranged signal to gently alert your spouse that you can take over. Discuss potential scenarios in advance, so if your husband is eyeball to eyeball with your son, you can go up and put a hand on his shoulder to signal that he needs to take a step away and calm down. As a warning, if you are the one engaged in an argument with your child that's going nowhere fast, and you feel the gentle pat on your shoulder, don't turn around in rage, rip your shirt in half like any good wrestler, and yell, "I've got this; back off!" That defeats the purpose of the tag-team plan.

- Most importantly, if you and your spouse disagree on how to handle your child's behavior, you should never discuss this in front of your child—period. Realize that when one parent undermines the other parent in this way, it hurts both parents. That's because your child is going to question both of you. Sometimes, kids feel like they have to choose sides. Not only that, they're going to feel insecure that the two of you don't seem to know what to do because after all, if you knew what to do, you'd be agreeing. Therefore, these things have to be handled privately. That's another reason why a prearranged signal like a light touch on the arm is helpful. Or you can simply say to the other parent, "Can I talk to you upstairs for a quick minute?"

• Similarly, never undermine the other parent in an overt or subtle way. If you disagree with the way your spouse is handling things, support him or her in front of the kids and discuss it privately later.

These recommendations are even more important for divorced or separated parents. Kids and teens are quite adept at playing divorced parents against each other, but ultimately having one parent undermining or degrading the other hurts the children. If parents are subtly or overtly criticizing each other, the children often end up having shaky self-esteem or other emotional issues. Focus on the best interests of the kids, and agree to co-parent as a unified team, regardless of how you feel about each other.

GO TEAM: PRESENTING A UNIFIED FRONT

GO TEAM: PRESENTING A UNIFIED FRONT

7

Going the Distance:
Achieving Long-Term Success
and Avoiding Common Pitfalls

In my experience (as a child psychologist and as Mom), what are the biggest impediments to long-term success and consistency as a parent? Exhaustion and being way too busy are two of the most common culprits. So many of us are living life one hundred miles per hour and putting out whatever fire is blazing immediately in front of us. We come home from work or the kids arrive home from school, and we are already cross-eyed with exhaustion and most definitely not in the mood for anything difficult. It's a shame, in fact, that we live in a culture where being busy is worthy of bragging rights, and we see on social media the subtle (and in-your-face) announcements of one's prowess in multitasking or accomplishments in a day.

GOING THE DISTANCE

Self-Care

Because of this busyness and fatigue, we often go for the path
of least resistance. You may half-heartedly make a demand of
a child or lightly reprimand him or her for misbehavior, but
you and your child know your heart isn't in it and you won't
enforce it, and therefore it has no weight. "But how do I garner
strength and stick-to-it-iveness?" you ask. Let me take a quick
detour into a favorite topic of mine (especially for moms) called
self-care. Just because it has become the norm to skimp on
sleep, grab junk food, and avoid exercise in order to get some
much-needed veg time, it doesn't mean that's right. I fully know
that we can't achieve perfect physical, mental, spiritual, and
emotional balance every single day, but we can do better about
carving out essential time for exercise, sleep, healthy diet, and
mood-boosting activities on a regular basis. Here are some of
my favorite self-care tips:

1) Just do it! Yeah, I wish I came up with that. But seriously,
   when it comes to exercise, most success comes by planning
   when in your day you will exercise and how and then getting
   out there and doing it. I typically look at my calendar on
   a week-to-week basis and plan out when I will attend a
   spin class, go for a run, swim laps, or go to the gym. I don't
   exercise every single day, but I try to have more days than
   not that include some kind of activity. Even if I can't officially
   exercise, I try to drag my husband and kids out for an after-
   dinner walk to get in some steps and fresh air. Try taking the
   stairs instead of the elevator or holding walking meetings
   with coworkers or staff.

2) Establish a goal bedtime and work backward. If your goal
   bedtime is 11:00 p.m., plan your evening routine around
   that deadline. In other words, turn off devices and the TV at
   10 p.m. Then do your hygiene/bedtime routine including a

GOING THE DISTANCE

bath or shower. Finally, allow for fifteen or twenty minutes of reading, drawing, or any other quiet activity leading up to lights out.

3) Allow yourself to insert small daily and medium-ish weekly pleasurable activities. The go-to treatment for anxiety and depression is cognitive behavioral therapy (CBT). One of the key components of the behavioral piece is to add pleasurable activities to (or back to) your life. Pleasurable activities are often thrown by the wayside when we get stressed, depressed, anxious, or overly busy. But pleasurable activities are essential for your mental health and mood. Pleasurable activities I can personally recommend include the following:

- Watching sitcoms or reality shows on TV with your honey or your kids
- Reading a great novel
- Going on a walk in the neighborhood (Bonus points if you find wild berries or feed ducks or geese in a pond)
- Tending your garden (At my house, that translates to admiring the thriving mint and searching pointlessly for any vegetables.)
- Getting a pedicure or massage
- Grabbing coffee, lunch, or drinks with a friend
- Joining a book club, garage band, garden club, or any other group with whom you share a common interest
- Playing tennis, going on a run, or swimming
- Playing board games or cards with your kids
- Grilling out or trying a new recipe
- Snuggling with your spouse/partner or kids and watching a movie
- Blasting your favorite music and having impromptu dance parties
- Petting your cat or dog (In our house, we have four cats to choose from.) Believe it or not, there is science behind

the mental health benefits of loving on your pets—
it's linked with reducing stress and lowering your
blood pressure.

- Listening to live music, especially outdoor concerts in the summer
- Shopping with your sibs or friends
- Perusing social media (But careful—this one is a potential time killer.)
- Taking a bubble bath with a candle burning, a magazine to read, and a glass of something bubbly
- Sex. Enough said, and "You're welcome" to any fellas reading this.
- Volunteering: Giving back to others is another automatic "feel good" experience and is correlated with an enhanced mood and improved mental health.

GOING THE DISTANCE

4) Fine-tune the art of saying no. Women especially have self-imposed or society-imposed standards that pressure us to do it all. Therefore, when we are asked to volunteer on a committee at school, teach a class at church, or help a neighbor plan a graduation party, our first instinct is to say, "Sure, of course." While I am a fan of volunteering and charity work, I have learned it is to my own self-detriment and/or the detriment of my family to say yes to everything. As an added challenge, I love a lot of things and get excited about new opportunities. Therefore, I have learned that when presented with a new opportunity, I need to say five magical words, "Let me think about that." Next, in the quiet moments of the day, contemplate your current commitments, your priorities, your schedule, your genuine desire for this activity, and then decide yes or no.

5) Moderation is key! I do preach this quite a bit with my clients and friends. I love ice cream, fast food, pizza, and wine. However, I try to follow the 80/20 rule (or 70/30 on some days) and eat healthy-ish stuff most of the time, with indulgences taking up the other 20 or 30 percent. Many professionals observe that extreme diets and lifestyles that require eliminating food groups or giving up all "fun" food don't have the staying power of a moderate diet. If you are fueling your body with healthy foods, you will have more energy and feel better.

6) "You Gotta Have Faith." OK, again, I wish I came up with that one. But there are fairly well-established connections between faith, spirituality, and religion and health benefits. In addition to the peace of mind that comes with knowing we are not alone and having a deeper purpose, many studies have found that daily meditation and prayer leads to the "relaxation response": decreased metabolism, decreased

heart rate, decreased breathing rate, and slower and calmer brain waves. As a Christian, I have found my beliefs and awareness that God is with me have absolutely been buffers through tough times. In terms of parenting specifically, I have certainly found comfort in prayer in moments when I was simply overwhelmed by its demands or stressed by my children.

Subtle sabotages (Say that three times fast!)

If you are practicing self-care, you will have more energy for dealing with subtle sabotages sneaking into your day. There are hundreds of subtle behaviors children and teens engage in daily that erode your authority as a parent. As I elaborated on earlier, these behaviors tend to pick up momentum over time and devolve into much more egregious acts of disrespect as a child gets older. Again, because many parents are so exhausted and distracted, it's all too easy to let a snide comment or rude growl slide. When I have worked with families over time or seen a child off and on in therapy, I have observed that sassy tones and ugly looks morph into teens saying "F-U! You're not the boss of me!" It's critical to constantly monitor, address, and nip these smaller behaviors in the bud. Examples (which may have all been observed in my own home) include rolling eyes, making a mocking face, saying something in a sarcastic tone, interrupting, turning one's body away as the parent speaks, starting to walk away as a parent is talking, and saying "I know!" As tiring as it is, each and every offense needs to be addressed. Does that mean you give a punishment or consequence for every act? Not necessarily. But each nonverbal and verbal offense needs to be acknowledged.

When our kids were much younger, we were out to dinner at a restaurant with a big group. The table was set up with adults at one end and kids at the other. After ensuring our children had their food and reminding our little one to eat her vegetables, we engaged in conversation with our friends. As the meal was winding down and we were cleaning up, I noticed a suspicious amount of broccoli florets under Logan's chair. I quickly debated letting it go, as I didn't want a scene in front of others, but I knew this type of behavior had to be confronted. So I pulled Logan aside, discussed with her why she had dropped broccoli on the floor, and gave a consequence of having more vegetables when we got home.

Let's peek at the Goodman family. Twelve-year-old Sara has just sauntered in from a friend's house and immediately throws her bag on the floor, collapsing on the couch with her phone. Her mom says, "Sara, please pick up your bag and go through your chore list before you get on your phone."

Sara, still staring at her phone, sighs and says in a rude, exasperated tone, "Argh, Mom! I am just peeking at my texts for like two minutes, geez!"

Mom walks over to Sara, bends over to make eye contact, and responds, "Sara, look up at me. You can't speak to me that way. You know the rules around your phone. Hand it to me, and once you are done with your chores, you can have it back." Sara then moans, "Oh my gosh, seriously? Why are you so strict?" as she furiously types to finish a text. Mom calmly replies, "Sara, I asked you to stop speaking rudely, and you didn't obey, so now you lose your phone for an hour."

Yay, Mrs. Goodman! Although in that scenario, she did give the behavior a consequence, it is sometimes enough to verbally correct it.

We observe a different scene in the Bueno family. Ten-year-old

Marco is struggling with math homework at the kitchen table. As Dad passes by, he states, "Hey, buddy, looks like you're having a tough time. You OK?"

Marco throws his pencil down, whining, "What do you think? You know I hate math!"

Dad hands his pencil back and responds, "Hey, that's not a nice way to talk to me. I was just checking on you. Please speak more respectfully, even when you're upset."

Marco looks up and states, "I know, Dad. I'm sorry. I'm just frustrated with this worksheet." Dad then joins Marco at the table, and they work on the sheet together.

Remember, the end goal is not to have a respectful five-minute exchange with your child, although that is quite nice. The end goal is to have a teen and young adult who automatically chooses his or her words carefully, is aware of body language and tone of voice, and responds respectfully. The bonus is that those now-ingrained behaviors automatically make your child a nicer person to go out into the world at large. Not only will your relationship with him be better, but he will also automatically respond to teachers, bosses, and peers in a kind and respectful manner.

GOING THE DISTANCE

GOING THE DISTANCE

8

Dealing with Technology

Tweens, Teens, and Screens (I did make that one up!): What to do? Parents of tweens and teens often struggle to keep up with technological and social networking advances. When it comes to monitoring their children's activities, they aren't sure what's acceptable and what's intrusive. Often, because of the confusion, they end up assuming their kids are navigating the technological and social networking waters appropriately. This is often an incorrect assumption. With the recent rash of teacher-student sex scandals and teen bullying, it is all too apparent that parents can never be too cautious or too involved in their kids' lives. The show 13 Reasons Why highlights how a harmful message gone viral can do significant and sometimes permanent damage to a teen's reputation, emotional health, or life. It's also important to remember that research now shows the brain doesn't finish developing until the mid-twenties. (This fact amazes me when I consider that my husband I married at ages twenty-three and twenty-four!) An undeveloped brain can't always see the big picture, conjure up consequences to actions, understand their future impact, or effectively plan. Therefore, trusting a child or teen with a powerful device that can disseminate information to friends, family, or the world with one tap of a finger is actually a big decision not to be taken lightly.

We like to think we hold some type of modern-era record as our daughter Zoe made it through middle school without a phone! Although she did remind us at times how she was the only one in her class without a phone, she was actually a very good sport about it most days, and she did have the ability to text some with her iPad. She just got her first phone with Instagram for her fourteenth birthday, right before entering high school. However, that decision was largely driven by our need to communicate with her now that she is more active and independent, running cross country, seeing friends, and going to church activities. Although we did feel somewhat alone in our decision to wait to give our daughter a phone and social media access, there is growing support among similarly minded parents. There is a

very exciting movement toward parents waiting until at least eighth grade to give their child a smartphone, emphasizing that if this becomes the new norm, it will unite parents: **www.westportmoms.com/wait-until-8th-pledge**

Although my personal and professional opinion is to hold off as long as you can before handing over any device with a means to connect with the world, I understand the realities of our world are that most kids will have a phone or device by middle school, if not before. Therefore, let me arm you with my top dos and don'ts to survive this technology-saturated world with your kids safe and healthy.

Do:

- Have your tween's and teen's passwords to everything— e-mail, phone, voicemail, Facebook account, and so on. There should be a family rule that you have the right to access these accounts at any time. You likely paid for the phone and pay for the monthly service, so it is your property.

- Routinely ask your child or teen to hand over his or her phone for you to scan the text messages to make sure everything is on the up and up. It's OK to check messages when they aren't aware as well.

- Create and enforce rules for technology. When should children and teens shut down their laptops and cell phones each night? (Yes, there should be a designated time to shut down devices and get them out of the room.) When are they allowed to surf the net or hop on social media? What misbehaviors cause them to lose these privileges?

- Become friends or followers with your children on Facebook, Instagram, Snapchat or whatever social media they are on. If they deny your request, let them know it goes along with the privilege of having a social media account, and promise you won't post any embarrassing pictures of them or make cheesy comments on their posts.

- Have children charge their devices outside their rooms each night. It is best for devices to be charged in a public area such as the living room, or in your bedroom if you have concerns that your children may sneak and go searching for the phone

DEALING WITH TECHNOLOGY

in the night. Charging devices outside their rooms serves two purposes. First, it allows you to check their posts and texts and ensure they are appropriate. And research shows that the blue light emitted by screens suppresses melatonin, the hormone that naturally makes us sleepy at night. Therefore, if your child has her face in an iPad or phone right up until bedtime, she may have trouble falling asleep. Best advice is to remove all screens (even TV and computers) at least an hour before bed. Wait, what? Yes, I hear it too. Your teen is complaining, "But I have to have the alarm on my phone" or "But I listen to music on my phone as I am going to sleep." Hmmm. Although those are compelling reasons, we can give children and teens alarm clocks and (hold on, I had to go look in a history book and remind myself of this one) radios, CD players, or MP3 players if need be.

Don't:

- Only look for obviously inappropriate messages from other adults or kids—look for subtle messages that might indicate your child or teen is being cyberbullied or led into an inappropriate relationship with a teacher or coach. I have a twelve-year-old client who gets very vicious and nasty messages from her best friend. She has read me various text strings, and I have been horrified at the manner in which her BFF communicates with her. Her BFF criticizes her or hounds her when she doesn't agree with her decisions, she questions her when she doesn't believe her, and she makes mild threats about spending time with other friends. Even subtly abusive texts like these can do significant emotional damage and need to be discussed openly with your child.

- Assume because your home computers have security settings that your savvy teens will be safe. Double check the history of Internet use regularly and regularly change passwords on computers you don't want them to have access to.

- Take anything at face value. These days, clever kids have found ways to have secret photo vaults buried under innocent-looking calculator icons. They may have two social media accounts—a fake one that has only innocent posts and a real one with more questionable content. Strive to stay one step ahead constantly. Attend workshops on technology, do regular Google searches to find the newest ways teens can manipulate and deceive using technology, and have open discussions with other parents. I am always thrilled when I host my "Tweens, Teens, and Screens" workshop, because parents always end up sharing new ideas and tips with one another and with me. Ask other parents and school staff, "What are you seeing these days with your child or student's social media, phone, electronics? What is new?"

    - I had a fifteen-year-old client who was a master manipulator when it came to phones and technology. Although her mom was on the ball enough to track her whereabouts, she had determined how to turn off her phone tracking so she could go places her mom would not approve of. When she was grounded from her phone, she would borrow a friend's phone that she kept hidden. She also had secret photo vaults that contained photos of drinking and drug use and sexual references.

- Be naïve. Don't think that because your child is making good grades and is well behaved that he or she is necessarily staying out of trouble. Being involved in their lives face to face as well as their technological and social networking lives is essential to good parenting these days. Have regular check-ins about how school is going, what is new in her social group, what her biggest stressor is, and how she's feeling.
- Avoid confrontation. If you see a post or read a text that even mildly nags at your parental instincts, address it immediately. It is always better to err on the side of caution than to assume it's nothing and realize too late your child or teen was caught

DEALING WITH TECHNOLOGY

up in something dangerous or unhealthy.

- Feel guilty for caring and checking and double checking and triple checking or for posting occasional shout-outs to your kids on social media, so they know you are watching, and their peers know, too. You are genuinely being a good parent by being actively involved in their lives, and their electronic and technological lives are no exception.

When can technology be too much?

There has recently been more attention given to the fact that gaming and/or Internet use can be an addiction. In fact, there is a cutting-edge program in Seattle called ReSTART focused on gaming and Internet addiction (**www.netaddictionrecovery. com**). Although the current Diagnostic and Statistical Manual of Mental Disorders, 5th edition (DSM-5) does not include an official diagnosis for Internet Gaming Disorder (IGD), it is listed in the section on conditions for further study (APA 2013).

Where do parents start differentiating between normal gaming and Internet use, which is usually pretty intense to begin with, and usage that is problematic?

1. Know the warning signs of a possible addiction or excessive screen use.
- Playing for increasing amounts of time
- Thinking about gaming during other activities
- Gaming to escape from real-life problems, anxiety, or depression
- Lying to friends and family to conceal gaming
- Feeling irritable when trying to cut down on gaming
- Becoming socially isolated—dropping out of social networks and giving up other hobbies

2. Implement strategies to find a balance for the necessary evil of screens and technology.

DEALING WITH TECHNOLOGY

- Parents can model effective "media diets" to help their children learn to be selective and healthy in what they consume. Take an active role in children's media education by viewing programs with them, checking their phones, watching the games they play, checking their Internet histories, and so on.

- Be a good role model. Don't check your phone at every stoplight or check Facebook every time you hear the ding.

- Make a media use plan, including mealtime and bedtime curfews for media devices. Screens should be kept out of kids' bedrooms as much as possible.

- Limit entertainment screen time to less than one or two hours per day. In children under two, discourage screen media exposure.

- Build a reward system about screens. Set rules about screen times on school days and non–school days with rewards for cooperation and consequences for noncompliance or arguing, and enforce them consistently.

- Consider using electronic TV-time monitors or apps that monitor and budget screen time. (See resources section below.)

- Build in other types of daily activities—family walks, games, reading, and so on.

- Have meals without the TV on—make mealtime family time. Don't allow any eating of snacks or meals in front of the TV.

- Stop screen time thirty minutes to an hour before bedtime to reduce the excitation of the brain before sleep.

- Have screen-free days—maybe one day a week—and have screen-free times each day.

DEALING WITH TECHNOLOGY

- Talk to your children about being good digital citizens, and discuss the serious consequences of online bullying. If your child is the victim of cyberbullying, it is important to take action with the other parents and the school if appropriate. Attend to children's and teens' mental health needs promptly if they are being bullied online, and consider separating them from the social media platforms where bullying occurs.

- Make sure kids of all ages know that it is not appropriate or smart to send or receive pictures of people without clothing or sexy text messages, whether they are texting friends or strangers. Many teens and parents don't realize there are legal ramifications to receiving a text with naked or sexual images, even if you didn't ask for it.

- If you're unsure of the quality of the media diet in your household, consult with your children's pediatrician about what your kids are viewing, how much time they are spending with media, and privacy and safety issues associated with social media and Internet use.

DEALING WITH TECHNOLOGY

What if you think it is an addiction?

- See a child/adolescent psychologist who can work with you and your child to assess the situation and implement helpful interventions.

- Even if you're not sure it's an addiction, if you think screens are causing problems, try a "detox" in which the child or the entire family goes for a period of time with no screens.

Resources

- Circle Go (**www.meetcircle.com/circle-go**) allows parents to manage all their kids' devices with one app, including establishing time limits and bedtimes and monitoring how they spend their time online.
- NEW AAP guidelines came out October 2016. You can create your own online family media plan at **www.healthychildren. org/English/media/Pages/default.aspx**.
- As monitoring apps are constantly changing, it's best to google "best apps for monitoring child's phone/electronic use" to get the most up-to-date recommendations.
- The following is a sample family media pledge. Use it as a starting point, and modify as needed for your family's needs. The goal is to incorporate technology into our lives in a meaningful way that allows us to have a healthy balance of online and off-line time.

Family Time Media Pledge
Kids and teens:

- I will never give out personal information online or by text and will avoid all chat rooms except ones my mom and dad have looked at and approved.
- I understand my parents have a right to check into my media history on my computer, phone, other devices such as iPod Touch, games, and whatever else I use regularly. I will keep my total screen time to two hours a day except when doing a project for school or when my parents give me permission.
  - I will not watch shows or play games that are inappropriate for me or for friends and family watching or playing with me.

DEALING WITH TECHNOLOGY

Parents:

- I will check what my kids are doing online and on their phones, consider using parent controls, and use them judiciously.
- I will let my kids know that I will be checking their computers and phones and enabling parent controls on their computers and gaming units.
- I will take the time to be interested in what my kids are doing online and in the digital world and talk to them about that world.
- I will help them make good media choices.
- If my child makes a mistake, I will ask questions and learn what happened before I punish or take away technology.
- I will take away technology as a consequence for breaking family rules for technology OR abusing a privilege.

Entire family:

- We will talk as a family at one meal a day with no technology in sight.
- We will agree to technology-free times such as meals, weekends, and vacations.
- We won't sacrifice important family time for media or digital use of any kind. If media gets in the way, we need to recognize we are using it too much or in a way that is not helping our family.
- We agree to use technology responsibly by not
  - Texting or talking on a cell phone while driving.
  - Using cell phones in a public location where it may annoy others.
  - Using technology to harm others by engaging in bullying or slanderous actions.
  - Listening to music with earbuds in a manner that prevents us from hearing passing cars or pedestrians and never while driving.

DEALING WITH TECHNOLOGY

Family Time Media Pledge

We agree to follow the tenets and abide by the rules described in our Family Media Pledge.

Date: _____

Signed: Parents: _____

_____

Kids and teens: _____

_____

_____

_____

DEALING WITH TECHNOLOGY

9
The Softer Side of No Wimpy Parenting

If you have been a fan of No Wimpy Parenting for a while, you know we are usually all about "Take back your power!" "Start a revolution," or "You have the authority!" The *Rocky* theme song is what I like to walk out to at workshops, for crying out loud!

But that doesn't mean that effective parenting only relies on stronger willpower, a take-charge attitude, and a no-nonsense mentality. In order to have not only your kids' respect, but also healthy and close relationships with them, you have to invest in the softer side of parenting. Even with teens. Even with (gasp) *middle schoolers!*

How do we develop the warm and fuzzy part of our relationship with our child or teen without becoming wimpy? The simple answer is that it's all about time and intention. Yes, we have all heard it preached that quality time is important. But some clichés are there for a reason...they work! Many of us are parenting at the speed of light. We wake up with a jolt in the morning and try to remember what day it is and who has to be where and when. Then the day is a blur of our work and racing kids around to school, sports, lessons, and so on. (For a visual of this, please see the hilarious scene in Bad Moms where the poor mom is multitasking—driving and eating spaghetti at the same time—and hilarity ensues.) When we come home, it's making dinner, prodding kids to do homework and chores, reminding them to shower, and then collapsing in a heap when the kids are finally in bed. It's a challenge to find time to breathe or take care of yourself, let alone to carve out that quality time everyone talks about.

However, I encourage you to dogmatically insist on getting that time with your kids or teens every day or at least most days. It doesn't have to be going to a pottery painting studio (although those are fun) or grabbing a Frappuccino at Starbucks (although kids and teens do love that, too). I'm talking about finding fifteen minutes a day to truly connect with your offspring. What can that look like? Here are a few pointers:

THE SOFTER SIDE OF NO WIMPY PARENTING

- When you're stuck in the car, instead of your child having his or her face in a device and you sneaking peeks at your phone at the stoplights, consider turning on your kid's favorite radio station and then asking what was the best part of his or her day, what was the craziest thing that happened, or what his or her friends stressing out about these days (a sneaky way to learn about how they are feeling). Child development experts know that kids and teens are much more likely to chat with you if you are both staring ahead, rather than making them sit across from you and having that painful eye contact. Boys in particular often communicate better if they are engaged in an activity, or have something to do with their hands, like the omnipresent fidget spinners. Speaking of which...

- Ask (or make) your child take a quick walk with you around the block. This is another way to get that side-by-side time that is effective for connecting with tweens and teens. Even though my kids may grumble if I insist on this, it's amazing how quickly they loosen up when we're walking in the sunshine, birds are chirping, and I am an audience eager to hear all about their lives.

- On that note, you should aim to become an expert on your child. From personal experience, I know when a friend or acquaintance remembers what I am into, asks me about myself, or follows up on something I told them, I feel much closer to him or her. Let's remember that teens and toddlers are the most self-centered creatures on the planet, and it's OK; it's the natural state of those developmental phases. Therefore, if you make note of what kind of music he likes, what sports teams he's fanatical about, her current crush, her latest friend drama, or her most challenging class and then check in about these topics, your child and

THE SOFTER SIDE OF NO WIMPY PARENTING

teen will soak up the fact that you really care.

• Make bedtime snuggles a sacred nightly ritual. Yes, even your snarly teens have a drastic increase in snuggly-ness and sweetness if you get them on their backs tucked in with covers, and you push your way into the bed to lie beside them for a bit. I'm amazed at how even after a rough day, my fourteen-year-old will ask for me to lie with her while she is reading if I've started rubbing her arm or chatting about her day. If you have older teens who really don't want you in their beds, you can always wander into their room at bedtime, sit in a chair close by, and engage in chitchat as they are winding down for the night. But remember....

• Kids need physical affection like they need water, food, and shelter. Therefore, don't give up on them during those awkward tween or teen years, when they seem as bristly as porcupines. Per Virginia Satir, a respected family therapist, "We need four hugs a day for survival. We need eight hugs a day for maintenance. We need twelve hugs a day for growth." What a challenge for us parents. That means we need to start the day off by grabbing our kid for a hug as they stumble into the kitchen for breakfast and sneak in another as they go out the door, another as they come home from school, and another at bedtime. But that's only four! Remember that other creative ways to give that affection are kissing the top of their heads as they do homework, putting an arm around them if they are struggling with an assignment, and squeezing a hand as they walk with you. Even giving a high five wins some physical affection points.

• Remember the power of positive words. As parents, we can often find ourselves only barking out criticism for what our kids did poorly or not at all or complaining about their behavior or attitudes. I often share with my parent-coaching clients the analogy of a nice boss and a mean boss. If you have a boss who only criticizes you, tells you you're not doing it right, and is negative with you, how motivated are you to do excellent work or to spend time with that boss? Not very, right? But, if you have a boss who praises your strengths, encourages you, and tells you how much he or she appreciates having you on the team, aren't you highly motivated to work hard and to spend time with that boss? Kids and teens are like that. They need to hear our words of encouragement, what we love about them, and how we appreciate their efforts. Try to say at least a few positive things to your kids every day.

- Forced family fun (FFF): It is critical to carve out family time or one-on-one time with your kids and teens. I developed FFF as a way to ensure all four of us would know this is sacred time carved out to watch a movie together, go out to eat, hang in the backyard and toss the football, or go hiking on nature trails. If you establish FFF when kids are young, they won't resist as much when you announce, "OK, guys, make a note. Friday night, it's FFF; don't make any plans." (As a bonus, if you plan FFF on a Friday, it becomes FFFF, and that's just even more wonderful!)

- Quick and easy one-on-one fun time ideas: challenge your kids or teens to a friendly game of UNO (or another card game), ping pong, or hangman in the downtime after dinner before they run off to their rooms again.

- Drop everything and respond (DEAR): Here is what I have learned about tweens and teens in particular: bonding with them has to come on their timing. When I have carved out time in my schedule to spend with the kids, it is often in contradiction to what they want to be doing right then and there. Although many times I still insist on spending that time with them (see FFF), I have learned they are much more talkative and warm if it comes at their initiative. Of course, this means my daughters may come up to me to chat or ask questions when I have finally settled in front of the computer to work. Or when I'm snuggling with my youngest at night, dreaming of my "me time" and planning my escape from her room, Logan might throw a leg around me and beg, "Will you please just snuggle a few more minutes?" Sigh.

The glass of Pinot or new book can wait. If you want to connect, you have to turn away from the laptop (closing it is even better), drop what you're doing, make eye contact, and say, "Tell me about it!" or "Sure, I'll snuggle a few more minutes." As I was in the final caffeine-laden, sleep-deprived hours of finishing this book, Zoe stumbled downstairs early in the morning as she was getting ready for high school. She was in a friendly and chatty mood and started talking about her plans for her fourth book. Although I had to do some quick mental gymnastics, I spun my chair around, looked into her excited eyes, and engaged in a discussion about plans for her book.

If you want to establish the foundation of a loving relationship that will have your kids seeking you out when they are adults and don't have to give you the time of day, you have to accept every nugget of time and attention given to you and savor it like a rare jewel.

OK, so instead of the *Rocky* theme song, imagine a lilting soothing melody...one of those with the sounds of ocean waves in the background. And then get yourself in a soothing, loving frame of mind, and go find that kid or teen of yours and find a way to connect, touch, or encourage!

10
Success Stories

One of my favorite cases to see at my private practice is parent-coaching clients. Even better is when they have already heard of my No Wimpy Parenting approach, and they are foaming at the mouth to get started. In order to highlight how any family can benefit from these tips, I thought I would give a quick taste of two families I was privileged to work with and to witness their successes firsthand. (Of course, the identifying details have been changed to maintain confidentiality.)

Family 1: The France family
Remember the seven-year-old with the potty mouth and the clever parents who added ZTB to my CWC? That is the France family. After eight No Wimpy Parenting coaching sessions with me, the transformation in this family was unbelievable. During the intake, parents described their concerns for Caleb, their seven-year-old. In addition to his cursing (the really bad words, not just "poopy head"), they were concerned about his explosive temper, chronic negativity, refusal to try certain activities, and defiance toward his parents. When asked what discipline

methods they were currently using in the home, Mr. and Mrs. France said they "sometimes" yelled, took away privileges, tried time-out, or sent Caleb to his room, and they had attempted a token system in the past. Upon further discussion, it seemed that, like many parents, these guys knew some of the tools to use but weren't using them consistently or effectively. No Wimpy Parenting to the rescue.

Early on, we established the importance of giving warnings, and these parents learned about CWCs. After only one week of using CWCs, this couple came back in to report they were delighted and amazed that their children were mastering "first time, every time" obedience, one of the tenets I teach for first-time compliance. After combining CWCs with the ROCKS system, things really took off! The France family was quite motivated to make a change and decided to have weekly meetings on Sunday to discuss the ROCKS system and any other strategies they were implementing with the kids. As I recommend, they were constantly fine-tuning and revising ROCKS to keep it engaging and motivating for the kids. Caleb quickly got excited about earning rocks, especially as he was saving up for an outing to a local arcade. Mr. and Mrs. France also adopted ZTBs (zero-tolerance behaviors) with respect to Caleb's cursing—in other words, he immediately lost a privilege or had another consequence any time he cursed. After five sessions, the parents reported Caleb's cursing had been eliminated altogether. He just didn't curse anymore. They also reported each week how delighted they were with the overall shift in Caleb's negative attitude and angry outbursts.

Because these parents were motivated and creative, they made the ROCKS system their own by adding various levels of rewards with slogans, in addition to adding the Golden Rock... rock...rock...(Imagine an echo after this is said.) They painted

SUCCESS STORIES

one large rock gold and decided to save it to give to one of their children each week for achieving an especially exciting behavior milestone or for getting a certain number of regular rocks. Over time, the Golden Rock evolved as a competition among siblings and was given for a combination of good character, helpfulness in the family, and behavior. The Golden Rock could be cashed out for special one-on-one outings with the parents or for cool toys. This creativity kept the ROCKS system fresh and exciting and also embraced the idea of bonus rocks, which I encourage to reward children for positive behaviors that aren't in the official ROCKS system. Caleb's parents also added sportsmanship to his ROCKS goals and began reinforcing good sportsmanship as he tried sports again. Overall, Caleb's parents reported much success with remaining calm instead of yelling, eliminating repeated requests and empty threats, having a straightforward reward system, and having zero tolerance for egregious behaviors. (Note: Because Caleb had autism and therefore had other social and emotional challenges, he was enrolled in individual therapy and a social skills group at some points in our parent coaching. This trifecta was also quite effective in reinforcing the positive behaviors and having good accountability for the parents.)

Family 2: The Brazil family

The Brazil family had three boys, ages thirteen, ten, and eight. While their concerns originally centered around the middle son, Drew, we ended up getting a three-for-one, with the No Wimpy Parenting strategies helping with all the kids. During the initial sessions, the parents described concerns with Drew's meltdowns, his defiance, and his disrespectful behavior toward them, especially his mother. Drew's parents recognized he also struggled with anxiety and ADHD and that he and his mother butted heads frequently because they were wired similarly. Drew was a master at pushing his mother's buttons and would engage her in long, drawn-out arguments that usually ended with both yelling and/or crying. In an early session, his mother reported an incident in which Drew became very "sassy" while playing video games. His mother yanked the controller from his hands, yelled at him, and sent him upstairs. In another incident early on, the parents described letting Drew stay up late to watch a movie, after which he refused to go to bed. While acting out, he lay on the family dog and grabbed her tail. This act enraged his parents and set off a chain reaction of his parents physically carrying him to bed, Drew locking himself in his bathroom, Drew hitting his father, and Drew being yelled at and spanked by his mother. His mother was often teary in sessions, describing how she constantly felt angry and overwhelmed in her own home and carried a constant sense of defeat on her shoulders. Although in the early sessions, Mr. and Mrs. Brazil were very frustrated and had little hope things could change, we slowly but surely started making changes for the better.

First, we implemented the ROCKS system for all three children. We focused on reinforcing the desired positive behaviors; as with many families, the Brazil family had become accustomed to only punishing and reprimanding the negatives. Next, I encouraged the parents (either one, but even better if it could be both) to give each child twenty minutes of special time a day. As we discussed earlier, parents often become the mean boss and lose sight of the importance of nurturing the positive aspects of their relationships with their children. Children thrive on that individual attention, especially if parents follow the instructions to refrain from rules, reprimands, commands, and so on during the special time. The special time is child led (the child chooses the activity) and meant to be a low-key opportunity to spend time together. During special time, the parent refrains from criticizing, questioning, and requests and rather aims to be a pleasant spectator or narrator (e.g., "Oh it looks like you're building a pirate ship with your Legos. I think I'll work on making a treasure chest if that's OK").

After we had the ROCKS system and daily special time going, we integrated CWC and focused on the do's and don'ts of earning and losing privileges. In order to wipe out the cycle of Mom getting sucked into long verbal battles with a ten-year-old, I taught her the art of walking away and allowing the child to save face. She learned that if she had explained the consequence or her decision and Drew was still arguing, she needed to simply walk away and engage in something else. If Drew followed her, she learned it was OK to go to her room or a bathroom and lock the door until the situation de-escalated. Finally, she realized that having a parent continue to stare a child down and wait for him to respond was a recipe for a strong-willed child to dig in his heels even harder. But if she gave the warning and then walked away, her son, left to his own devices, was much more likely to comply. The power struggle was removed. The walk-away technique also combines quite nicely with the second consequence tool.

To illustrate: Drew was having a very difficult day. He was rude and surly all morning to his parents, and they correctly used CWC, he lost his chance to go to the skateboard park that afternoon. At that point, Drew became further enraged and began throwing things and making a mess in his room. His mother calmly gave another warning for a new consequence. She told Drew, "If you don't stop throwing things immediately, you will not only lose the skateboard park, but you won't be attending hockey practice tonight." Instead of hovering at his door staring him down, she slipped into the hall so she could listen but not engage in a showdown. Mrs. Brazil heard Drew flop on his bed and sigh. She peeked in a minute later and saw him reading a comic book by his bed.

Although the Brazil family experienced the two-steps-forward-one-step-back phenomenon throughout this time, they began to see an overall shift toward positive behavior and attitudes in their home. The parents felt more unified as a team after implementing some strategies to overcome the divide, and the mother felt less bitter and angry all the time. These parents began to enjoy their children again, and as a bonus, Drew met his goals for his own therapy, as he had made such strides in his emotional regulation and behavior.

Although I could give many more examples, it is fair to say I have never met a family yet who did not benefit from the No Wimpy Parenting techniques. If you have made it to the end of this book and are bursting with excitement to implement these ideas in your home, there is great news! Not only do you have this book as a resource to turn to in tough times, but you now have access to the No Wimpy Parenting universe: including resources on the website, blogs, and customized coaching! Learn more in the resources section in the appendix.

I salute you for having the courage to make a change. Remember, we are all in this together, and you are now in a community of No Wimpy Parenting converts who support and encourage you. Go slap that bumper sticker on your car, and get ready for your family to experience transformation like you never imagined!

SUCCESS STORIES

Appendix:
No Wimpy Parenting Pledge, Resources, and Cheat Sheet

Ready to join the NWP club (or family, as we like to think of it)? Are you ready to officially banish the weak, squishy parenting muscles of the past and replace them with the bulging biceps of a No Wimpy Parent? Well, it's about time!

After you sign the pledge on the next page (or for dramatic effect, you can recite the pledge aloud in a dark room with a candle glowing and the *Rocky* theme in the background), send us a picture of your signed card and sign up for the No Wimpy Parenting e-newsletter. We promise we won't overload your inbox, and we won't try to constantly sell you something. We want to be an ongoing resource for you—to keep you up to date with the most cutting-edge parenting advice, tips, and research. You can also schedule a NWP consultation to get specific advice to help your beloved family. If you schedule a customized consultation, we will also send you...wait for it...drum roll... a No Wimpy Parenting bumper sticker to proudly slap on your family car.

THE No wimpy™ PARENTING PLEDGE

I, _____, pledge to banish any former wimpy-parent ways. I am empowered and motivated to establish the proper authority and power structure in my home. Although our child(ren) will know they are loved, they will also know without a shadow of a doubt that the parents are running the show! I aspire to be a No Wimpy Parent, and although I know perfection is never possible, I will try my best every day.

Signature _____

Date _____

APPENDIX

If you love our mission and want to show your support, we also have a variety of shirts, hats, coffee mugs, and bumper stickers. Check out our store at **NoWimpyParenting.com/shop**.

E-mail **info@nowimpyparenting.com** to join the NWP e-mail newsletter or to schedule a customized NWP consultation. Want great news? Mention discount code: **NWPbeliever** and you'll get 50% off of your first consultation! (Yes, I will ask you random questions from the book to make sure you really read it). 😃

APPENDIX

CWC: Command, warning, consequence

ZTB: Zero-tolerance behaviors

First time, every time!

It's OK if they cry; you are being a good parent!

Remember, your parenting tool kit is filled with the following:
- ROCKS
- Time-out
- Chores
- Removal of privileges
- Quality time

No power suckers! Avoid the following:
- Button pushing
- Negotiations
- Partial compliance
- Questioning
- Decision-making
- Ignoring

APPENDIX

About Dr. Kristen Wynns

Dr. Wynns is frequently sought out as an expert on child psychology and parenting issues for radio shows, TV news, magazines such as Carolina Parent, and TV shows such as My Carolina Today and Daytime. She was the relationship columnist for a national magazine, All You, and writes two parenting blogs. Dr. Wynns is the founder of a parenting website and resources called NoWimpyParenting.com. No Wimpy Parenting™ services are available to help parents struggling with behavior or discipline problems at home. Dr. Wynns is frequently invited to speak at parenting workshops at schools, churches, and businesses. Dr. Wynns likes to say she is doubly qualified to give parenting advice because she is not only a child psychologist but also the mother of two children, ages fourteen and eleven.

Dr. Wynns is a child and adolescent psychologist who owns a child/adolescent specialty private practice in Cary and North

Raleigh, North Carolina, called Wynns Family Psychology. She has an MA and a PhD in clinical psychology from the University of North Carolina at Greensboro. At Wynns Family Psychology, Dr. Wynns and her talented team provide therapy for kids ages three and up, parent coaching, and social skills groups and camps. They also provide psychological and psychoeducational evaluations for ADHD, autism, learning disabilities, and gifted. Dr. Wynns specializes in high-conflict divorce cases by offering co-parenting therapy, reunification therapy, therapy for children of divorce, and a full menu of custody evaluations.

See **WynnsFamilyPsychology.com**
or **NoWimpyParenting.com** for more information.
To subscribe to Dr. Wynns's blogs,
visit **www.NoWimpyParenting.WordPress.com**
and **www.KristenWynns.WordPress.com**.
Follow Dr. Wynns on Facebook **@WynnsFamilyPsychology**
and on Twitter **@NoWimpy**.

Please e-mail questions or feedback to Dr. Wynns
at **Kristen@WynnsFamilyPsychology.com**.

Made in the USA
San Bernardino, CA
16 August 2018